I Still

Want You

---◆---

THE CALL TO A

DEEPER

PLACE!

Encounter One

I Still
Want You

---◆---

THE CALL TO A
DEEPER PLACE!

DR. MATTIE NOTTAGE

I STILL WANT YOU
THE CALL TO A DEEPER PLACE

Published By:
Mattie Nottage Ministries, International
P.O. Box SB–52524
Nassau, N. P. Bahamas
Tel: (888) 825-7568 or (242) 698-1383
www.mattienottage.org

Unless otherwise indicated, all Scripture quotations are taken from the King James Version, biblegateway.com and The Amplified Bible ©1987 by the Zondervan Corporation and the Lockman Foundation, Grand Rapids, Michigan.

Cover design by: Beyond All Barriers Publications & Media Group
Edited by: Beyond All Barriers Publications & Media Group
Format and Interior design by: BEYOND ALL BARRIERS PUBLICATIONS & MEDIA GROUP
Copyright ©2015 by Mattie M. Nottage
All rights reserved.

Printed in the United States of America
First Printing: March 2015
ISBN-13: 978-0-9896003-6-1

DEDICATION

This book is dedicated to believers across the globe whose deep and desperate desire is for more of the presence of God.

It is my earnest prayer that you will find that place in God and, once you find it, your passion and pursuit will take you deeper still.

ACKNOWLEDGEMENTS

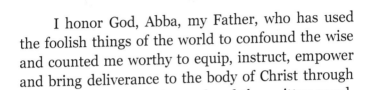

I honor God, Abba, my Father, who has used the foolish things of the world to confound the wise and counted me worthy to equip, instruct, empower and bring deliverance to the body of Christ through the preached, prophetic word and the written word. Without reservation, He will always be first in my life.

I thank God for my husband, spiritual covering and ministry tag team partner, Apostle Edison Nottage, our children and grandchildren. Their unwavering love, support and motivation inspire me to continue to be an available vessel for the Master's use.

Finally, I thank God for our congregation and spiritual sons and daughters around the world. Your desire to be taught and your desire for more of the presence of God push me to prepare you to embrace His presence. Deep calls unto deep...***I admonish you to go deeper!***

"I STILL WANT YOU!"
PROPHETIC RELEASE

◄►

Have you ever had dry seasons in your life and felt empty on the inside? Then the Spirit of God wrote this prophetic song, " I Still Want You," just for you.

For thus says the Spirit of Almighty God to you, today....

"..for I am lifting you from your place of drought and weariness says the Lord. I am bringing you from your place of spiritual famine and dryness to a new place of spiritual hunger. I see your thirst and can hear the desperation in your cry for me, says God. For even as the Deep calls unto the deep, even so am I calling you to my secret place.

I am placing within you a yearning and turning within your soul once again for me, says the Lord. Regardless of who and where you are right now, I love you my child and I know for a certainty that you love me too. Even as the deer longs for and goes after water, fearing for his own life, even so am I causing there to be a deeper desire to be birthed on the inside of you to want more and more of me.

I see your brokenness. I see your tattered, unwashed garments of shame and guilt. I see how your soul has been torn in fragments and how you are finding it difficult to cope. I see your hurt and understand the depth of your suffering by reason of all that has happened to you. My child I hear, I see and I know all about you and, in spite of what you are going through right now, you are still pursuing and coming after me.

"I STILL WANT YOU!"
PROPHETIC RELEASE CONT'D...

It seems as if the closer you come to me, the more I can smell the stench of burning flesh. I understand the depth of your hurt and unlike anyone else, I understand what it cost you to even be alive today. Your storms of hardship, your nights of heart-wrenching pain have all come up before me. I know the place where you are. I see your sacrifice.

Please know, my child, that my Grace is sufficient for you. I have paid the price for every tear drop you have shed. I have paid the price for you. Your debts are cancelled. Your name has been changed!

Let go of everything that is holding you back from me. As you give yourself wholly to me, I want you to know that I do not see your weaknesses, I see your strength. I do not see your sins, I see your need for me. I look beyond your failures, mistakes and foolish pitfalls. I embrace you with the warmth that only a true Father can give to His child.

Your season of demonic torment is over, and from this day forward you will hear my voice calling you in the night. You will hear my whispers beckoning you to take flight and fly with me in realms of glory beside still waters. I will cause you to walk through supernatural doors of opportunity. I will cause you to soar and fly to higher places in me where the greater revelation of Who I am will be unveiled to you.

"I Still Want You!" will become your mantra and anthem of songs for almost every season of our walk together. I love you with an everlasting love,..." says the Spirit of God.

TABLE OF CONTENTS

CHAPTER ONE

GIVE ME A DRINK...
I THIRST!

THE BECKONING

I believe that there is a time in everyone's life when the Holy Spirit draws you closer to God. While there is an initial drawing for salvation I believe that, as you begin to grow and mature in the things of God, there is also further drawing for a deeper level in Him. This is what I refer to as, ***the beckoning, a call to the deeper place.***

The Spirit of God will move upon your heart, causing you to desire intimacy with Him. He provokes you to leave your dry place of that which is wearisome and mundane, causing you to follow Him to a realm beyond the corridors of your flesh and human experience. You may begin to feel a deeper longing and desire for His presence, and you may even be compelled to embrace Him through your worship.

⁶ Jesus saith unto him, I am the way, the truth, and the life: no man cometh unto the Father, but by me. (John 14:6)

The beckoning is never physical or carnal; rather, it is a spiritual encounter that is wrought ***by*** the Holy Spirit ***in*** your spirit. Your heart is stirred as an overwhelming sense of finding God consumes your mind. You are then compelled to follow Him, driven by a deep yearning to be where He is, even if it is in the midst of a storm.

"Bid Me To Come!"

The disciples were in the midst of a storm in the middle of the ocean. They feared for their lives, only to see what appeared to be Jesus walking on the water.

Peter called out to Him and said, *"Lord if it is you, bid me to come."*

Jesus said, *"It is I, come!"*

"Come" is one of the most powerful words you will ever hear from the Spirit of God. It is the call for you to draw nearer to the One, True God who has created you.

44 No man can come to me, except the Father which hath sent me draw him: (John 6:44)

When Peter heard Jesus' voice bidding him to come, he stepped out of the boat onto the water and began walking in a realm that he never walked in before. He walked on something he should have sunk in, defying the laws of nature.

Heeding the call to come into the presence of the Almighty rewards you with limitless, supernatural blessings. Your experiences are profound and can only be summarized by the words ... *He called and I came!*

THE CALL TO A DEEPER PLACE

I believe that one of the greatest love stories told in the Bible is the one about King Ahasuerus and Queen Esther. This epic biblical romance was a "prophetic type" demonstrating the relationship that God desires to have with His people.

In the backdrop of this story, King Ahasuerus (Xerxes) planned a great feast and invited all of the nobles throughout the land to dine at his palace. There was much festivity, celebration and some revelry. The king brought out the finest wine and most delectable foods and everyone was enjoying the feast.

As the days of feasting wore on, King Ahasuerus wanted to display all of the glories of his royal palace, which included the beautiful Queen Vashti. *(Esther 1:11)*

He was a ruler to be honored, revered and admired for all of the splendor of his glorious kingdom. There was only one slight problem – when he called for Queen Vashti, she never came. In fact, she was adamant about not coming and made sure that all of the women agreed with her.

Although the king had called her she did not obey his voice because, first of all, she was having her own feast and, secondly, she did not want to be displayed as a "pawn" before the king's intoxicated friends. Operating in pride, arrogance and conceit she continued with her own banquet and refused to honor the king's request.

Dishonored and embarrassed before his entire court, King Ahasuerus vowed that he would never invite Vashti to come before his presence again. How could anyone dare deny the request or demand of the king? *(Esther 1:19–20)*

Vashti's refusal to honor the king's request not only brought shame to the king; it greatly offended the noble men of his court. She was very beautiful to look upon, however, in her spirit she was prideful, arrogant, conceited and rebellious. As a result, she no longer pleased the king and lost her position in his court.

The nobleman agreed with King Ahasuerus that Vashti should never come before his presence again and that another Queen should be sought out in Shushan to please the king.

One might ask, "How could anyone dare ignore the call of the king?" However, many people tend to operate in the same spirit of Vashti when they ignore the call of God to come before His presence in prayer and worship. At times when He is seeking to draw us closer to Himself, we generally offer excuses such as, "I am too tired" or "I am too busy."

I believe that, at some point and time in every believer's life, we will get the call to come to a deeper place in God. However, if we neglect to pray or read our Bibles we may miss the clarion call of the voice of God.

The Word of God says in **Ephesians 2:8–9**, that by grace we are saved through faith. In other words, we only qualify for the call because of the grace of God that has been given to us.

In return we are admonished to give God the honor that is due Him, according to **Romans 12:1–2** that is our *reasonable* service.

I beseech you therefore, brethren, by the mercies of God, that ye present your bodies a living sacrifice, holy, acceptable unto God, which is your reasonable service.

2 And be not conformed to this world: but be ye transformed by the renewing of your mind, that ye may prove what is that good, and acceptable, and perfect, will of God.

PREPARATION FOR HIS PRESENCE
"Favor – Fit For A Queen"

Due to the impropriety of the former Queen Vashti, King Ahasuerus issued a decree throughout all the land that he was seeking a new Queen who would come before him. No doubt the news spread like wildfire.

Every eligible young woman in the kingdom knew that she had an opportunity of a lifetime and the competition would be intense. She knew that she would have to endure the *process of preparation,* if she was going to win the king's heart. If you are going to receive favor from the King of kings you must be willing to endure the process of preparation.

The Turn of Esther

Can you imagine; Esther, a little orphan girl with no father or mother, but she has been given an opportunity to become the Queen? Her only requirement to obtain this honor was that she had to please the king. ***This could only be the favor of God on her life.***

Esther had to endure an arduous, extended purification process: "*...six months with oil of myrrh, and six months with sweet odours, and with other things for the purifying of the women.*" **(Esther 2:12)**

¹⁵ *Now when the turn of Esther,...was come to go in unto the king, she required nothing but what Hegai the king's chamberlain, the keeper of the women, appointed. And Esther obtained favour in the sight of all them that looked upon her.*

In the king's palace Esther received much favor and eventually won the position as the new Queen of Shushan. I believe that the natural purification process she endured was symbolic of the purification of her spirit. Esther's outer beauty may have caught the king's attention but I believe that it was her inner beauty that won his heart.

When your turn before the king comes absolutely nothing can stop you, especially when you have a pure heart.

***3 Who shall ascend into the hill of the LORD?
or who shall stand in his holy place?***

***4 He that hath clean hands, and a pure
heart (Psalm 24:3–4)***

Yes, God is looking for the pure in heart. I believe that these are the people who will begin to see the manifested glory of God like never before.

GIVE ME A DRINK...I THIRST!

**23 But the hour cometh, and now is, when
the true worshippers shall worship the
Father in spirit and in truth: for the Father
seeketh such to worship him.**

This is the hour where God is raising up a people who are thirsty and desperate for His presence and power. These are the people who are genuinely in search of the living God and do not wish to be given a watered down version of that which is authentic.

These people want to see the power of God in demonstration. They want the Christ in the fullest measure of His glory and are prepared to do whatever it takes to see and experience Him.

¹ O God, thou art my God; early will I seek thee: my soul thirsteth for thee, my flesh longeth for thee in a dry and thirsty land, where no water is;

² To see thy power and thy glory, so as I have seen thee in the sanctuary.

³ Because thy lovingkindness is better than life, my lips shall praise thee.

⁴ Thus will I bless thee while I live: I will lift up my hands in thy name.
(Psalm 63:1–4)

You cannot afford to serve God in a place where there is no water. The absence of water means the absence of spirit and life. As a believer, you can choose to remain in a dry dimension or spiritual satisfaction and delightful outpouring.

Water represents the presence of the Holy Ghost and God. If you find yourself in a place where there is no water, then it means that you are in a place where the Spirit of God is absent.

Staying in a place of perpetual dryness will only lead to spiritual death, and, can ultimately open the door to destruction and physical death.

God is calling you out of your state of spiritual dryness and is seeking to bring you to the new place, living and dwelling in the rich abundance of His presence.

According to Psalm 63, in order to satisfy your thirst, you must be prepared to:
1) Rise up early
2) Respond to the call
3) Make a decision to leave your dry place
4) Follow the leading of the Holy Spirit to the well
5) Drink from the Spirit of God regardless of who is looking.

WELLS OF LIVING WATERS
"Dig Again!"

Many people prevent themselves from experiencing the gushing force of the Spirit of God because they generally stop seeking if they do not "feel" anything. For the most part, they tend to dig once and then give up, not realizing that in the midst of their digging God is seeking to develop them spiritually.

Far too often some make the dreadful mistake of giving up during their season of drought and famine. It should be understood, beforehand, that pursuing God requires tenacity and a willingness to persevere regardless of what confronts you. This means having a mind made up to go beyond boundaries and limitations in order to discover a gushing well of living water.

> **¹² Then Isaac sowed in that land, and received in the same year an hundredfold: and the LORD blessed him. (Genesis 26:12)**

In **Genesis 26:12** the people of that day were experiencing one of the worst famines ever. However, Isaac sowed in that land in the same year and received a hundred-fold return. No matter who or what is fighting you, prepare yourself to push beyond it and contend for that which God has promised you.

Warfare At The Wells

> **¹⁸ And Isaac digged again the wells of water, which they had digged in the days of Abraham his father; for the Philistines had stopped them after the death of Abraham: and he called their names after the names by which his father had called them.**

19 And Isaac's servants digged in the valley, and found there a well of springing water.

20 And the herdmen of Gerar did strive with Isaac's herdmen, saying, The water is ours: and he called the name of the well Esek; because they strove with him.

21 And they digged another well, and strove for that also: and he called the name of it Sitnah.

22 And he removed from thence, and digged another well; and for that they strove not: and he called the name of it Rehoboth; and he said, For now the LORD hath made room for us, and we shall be fruitful in the land. (Genesis 26:18–22)

Isaac decided to dig the wells that his father had previously dug, but every time he did so the herdsmen of the land stopped them up. He then decided to shift his position and dug a third well elsewhere. This time they had no choice but to leave him alone.

Tenacity always pays off. If you keep digging you will eventually strike gold and your enemies will be forced to leave you alone.

The names of the wells that Isaac dug were:

1) **Esek** – which means strife and contention, because they strove with him

2) **Sitnah** – which means hatred, because they envied him and the way God was blessing him

3) **Rehoboth** – which means God has made room, because they did not contend with him for this well.

Whenever you come to a place in your life where you are willing to dig and dig again, God will enlarge you and make room for you. He will cause you to dig wells which will spring up as gushing wells of living water and spiritual or prophetic geysers which will bring health, wholeness and prosperity *(See more in Chapter 7).* Go after your spiritual wells and dig again, and again, if you have to. This prepares you for the meeting at the well.

THE MEETING AT THE WELL

The Spirit of God will rest in your life if you consistently dig deeper into the revelation of who He is. You eventually experience the profound phenomenon that is completely unforgettable.

This is a divine encounter which is reserved for those who are willing to take the time and "pay the price" to truly discover and rediscover the well of unlimited supply of the presence of God deep within their soul.

In John 4, when Jesus asked the woman at the well for a drink, she said that she had nothing to draw with. It was interesting that she had a receiving pot but did not bring a bucket with which to draw water. No one comes to the well with no apparatus to draw water.

This woman is a symbol of the modern day Church attendee who comes to the weekly church meetings only having the intention of participating in ceremonial, ritualistic programs and practices but having no desire to receive a fresh impartation from the Spirit of God.

These are the people who come empty and, most times, leave empty. They bring nothing to the well (no expectation of a move of God) but hope to connect with someone who brought their "something" to draw with. They are like the five foolish virgins who had no oil in their lamps when the bridegroom came.

[1]Then shall the kingdom of heaven be likened unto ten virgins, which took their

lamps, and went forth to meet the bridegroom.

2 And five of them were wise, and five were foolish.

3 They that were foolish took their lamps, and took no oil with them:

4 But the wise took oil in their vessels with their lamps.

5 While the bridegroom tarried, they all slumbered and slept.

6 And at midnight there was a cry made, Behold, the bridegroom cometh; go ye out to meet him.

7 Then all those virgins arose, and trimmed their lamps.

8 And the foolish said unto the wise, Give us of your oil; for our lamps are gone out.

9 But the wise answered, saying, Not so; lest there be not enough for us and you: but go ye rather to them that sell, and buy for yourselves.

10 And while they went to buy, the bridegroom came; and they that were ready went in with him to the marriage: and the door was shut.

11 Afterward came also the other virgins, saying, Lord, Lord, open to us.

12 But he answered and said, Verily I say unto you, I know you not.

13 Watch therefore, for ye know neither the day nor the hour wherein the Son of man cometh. (Matthew 25:1–13)

The Spirit of God is beckoning to you to move yourself from carnal, sensual, mundane dryness to a spiritual realm of being perpetually progressively drenched in who He is. He wants your depth in Him to be unreachable by the enemy, but you must have something to draw with. There must be something deep on the inside of your soul that is calling you to pursue Him.

In other words, there must be a hunger and thirst; a desire to experience God in greater ways which transcend natural pleasures and satisfaction.

"They that hunger and thirst after righteousness shall be filled." (Matthew 5:6)

Hunger speaks to the human need for food to satisfy an appetite or to receive nourishment and sustenance. On the other hand, thirst speaks to the need for water to refresh and replenish the body. The results of satisfying the need of being both hungry and thirsty is an energized, fully charged vessel that is ready to take dominion over all that has been entrusted to it.

GOD IS CALLING YOU DEEPER

The Bible says *my sheep know my voice.* When you receive the gift of salvation, your first prerogative is to be filled with the Holy Spirit. Once you become filled with the Holy Spirit (*new wine*) then you will gradually begin to understand what is the hope of His calling in you. You may not understand everything initially or in one encounter but, if you continue to pursue God, He will reveal Himself to you.

"The eyes of your understanding being enlightened; that ye may know what is the hope of his calling, and what the riches of the glory of his inheritance in the saints," *(Ephesians 1:18)*

The spirit of prophecy is the revelation of Jesus Christ. Once you get a revelation of who God is, it will change your entire life. No amount of religion, education, money or intelligence can help you to see the Christ for who He is. You are only able to recognize the Christ through the spirit of revelation as imparted only by the Spirit of God.

God must reveal Himself to you if you are ever going to know and embrace Him. The Bible clearly states that the things of the Spirit of God are foolishness to those who are carnal and ensnared by the things of the world such as religion, intellectualism, greed for money and the like. However, God reveals Himself to those who are spiritually discerning; who posture themselves to intimately know Him.

DEEP CALLETH UNTO DEEP

Deep calleth unto deep at the noise of thy waterspouts: all thy waves and thy billows are gone over me. (Psalm 42:7)

In **Psalm 42:7** the Psalmist David laments his desire for more of God. He poetically likens this desire to the need of a deer thirsting after a drink of water.

The deer is weary and thirsty after a long day's journey, but he knows that there is a lion nearby probably just as hungry after his long day's journey.   The deer's desperate thirst puts him in the precarious position of longing for just one sip of water from the brook that is calling him – to life or indeed to his death.

The hour of just being surface or borderline, on the shores of Christianity, is over. I believe that the Spirit of God is drawing those who are really hungry and thirsty for more of Him to a deeper level, to a brand new place.

The driving force behind this level of seeking is a deep seated hunger and a thirst that cannot be satisfied by anything else but the Spirit of The Almighty God. This hunger and longing drives you to a place of total surrender. In most cases this drive is a "solo" mission that those who are around you may not be aware of or understand.

When God is calling you to this level of intimacy, you may sometimes be misunderstood by the people around you. This deep place is beyond superficiality, mediocrity and mundane thinking. It is a new realm that is a mystery to many but a *"seekers heaven"* to those who will find it. It is a place of perfect glory, deep fellowship and intense intimacy with God.

Everyone should be in pursuit of this place. As Moses hid in the cleft of the rock and David dwelt in the secret place of the Most High, even so must we be drawn to the depth of the ocean in the spirit, seeking the face of God.

The Depth Of God's Presence

3 For I say, through the grace given unto me, to every man that is among you, not to think of himself more highly than he ought to think; but to think soberly, according as God hath dealt to every man the measure of faith. (Romans 12:3)

The Spirit of God spoke to me concerning spiritual measurement and how He has first given everyone two things:

1) A measure of grace
2) A measure of faith

As we yield to the Spirit of God we find ourselves relying more on this unfailing grace that we do not deserve but which has nonetheless, been extended to us.

Further, as we go deeper into the things of God, despite our many challenges and demonic warfare we understand that we all have been given a measure of faith. This faith, if truly realized, can awaken us to a realm of living in the supernatural every day.

In **Ezekiel 47** the Spirit of God takes him from waters to a river, then draws him, consequently from the brink of the river to waters measuring up to his ankle, knees, waist and eventually into waters he had to swim in.

The Brink Level represents individuals who tend to operate in uncertainty and doubt. The brink of the river is the land mass near its bank. Individuals at this place see everything on a logical, factual view point, exactly as it appears. They believe that there is a God, but refuse to fully embrace him as Lord. These people may struggle with a religious mindset.

And thou shalt command the priests that bear the ark of the covenant, saying, When ye are come to the brink of the water of Jordan, ye shall stand still in Jordan.
(Joshua 3:8)

The Ankle Level represents individuals who tend to carry various degrees of pride. They seek to operate in their own intellect or carnal knowledge. These people are not sure if they want to get wet and are stuck in a shoreline level of belief. They "splish/splash" around the things of God, content that they are a Christian and that's it! At this level, the slightest disappointment causes them to turn around and walk away. This is a place of superficial faith.

The Knee Level represents individuals who operate in a spirit of fear. The knees allow the body to bend the legs, and they represent flexibility. Therefore, persons at this level tend to be very unpredictable. One day they feel victorious and the next day they feel defeated. They are naturally very spontaneous or impulsive, and they tend to vacillate having mixed emotions. They always have lots of questions and concerns about moving further in the things of God. This is the "what if" level. "What if I step out and drown?" or "What if I try this and it does not work?"

Your personal trials and tribulations seem to be gnawing at you. Almost everything seems to be falling apart. Movement is very important at this level and, for whatever reason, you remain resolute, determined not to turn back. You then step to the next level.

The Waist Level represents individuals who have finally built up enough strength to launch further in the presence of God. They are not yet at the spiritual place where they should be, but they are closer than they were before. They are beginning to discern a greater level of the spirit of

God but are still somewhat hesitant to fully trust God. They are indecisive, wrestling with whether they "should surrender and turn back or push out a little further?"

At this level you find yourself further than you have ever been. Here, you can hardly hear the voices of the people on the shoreline *(people who are in your past or better yet, people who are far behind you)*. Instead, at this level, you are now hearing a different voice. Someone is now calling you from the ocean *(the deep).*

Stay focused! Do not begin to celebrate yet. Although you have moved further in His presence, you have not fully reached the place of surrender. Fear, pride and doubt are trying their utmost to hinder you. Also at this level you still have a degree of control. Although you believe God is able, you still find yourself relying on your human capabilities. You cannot depend on your physical strength to overcome at this level.

As you heed the call from the deep, you will have to spend more time in prayer, fasting and reading the Word. As you strive to release and go further, before you know it, you push off into the waters where you are now unable to stand.

This is the level where you should gird your loins with truth, focusing solely on the Word that God has spoken to you, and move forward.

Waters to swim in represent a place where you have never been before. It is a new dimension of spiritual courage where you are no longer in control but totally dependent on God. This is the place where the Spirit of God was trying to bring you where you fully trust Him.

At this level, the waves are billowing over you but you are still moving towards the deep. These are *uncharted waters*. You have never been this way before, everything seems strange and new.

In this place there is total trust and total faith. You are no longer able to stand, or depend on your ankles and knees to support you. There are no human powers at work here. All of your previous alliances are far behind you and you are now moving at the pace of the Holy Spirit; totally synchronized, moving hands and feet only as He directs you.

This is a place of intense worship, concentrated prayer, steadfast faith and supernatural expectations. Your measure of grace and faith are now working together to produce a "river-size" capacity destined for the deeper realm of God.

INCREASE MY CAPACITY FOR YOU

Capacity is the potential you have to accommodate, to hold, to contain and maintain what is being poured out into you. You may have been stretched beyond measure, in some cases beyond the measure that had previously been given to you.

This is, ultimately, the plan of God to increase your spiritual capacity to maintain a greater level of His glory. Deeper and deeper you find yourself drifting, certain of only one thing: your desire to experience Him in greater measures.

Remember in this hour that God is a "God of measurements". One of the laws of the kingdom clearly states that "Wherever there is a demand, there is a supply." If you desire more of God then ask Him to fill you with more of His presence. However, you must understand that fulfilling this request may require a process of stretching, pulling, drawing, measuring, molding and, above all...*humbling*.

The Deep has been designed for the "hungry, thirsty, desperate, dissatisfied, passionate, humble and above mediocrity" servant. These are those who are prepared to risk all, give all, and even lose all for a greater depth in God.

The Holy Spirit is moving through the body of Christ searching for those who are prepared to go deeper and further in Him. If you are willing to be stretched, demanding more from God; more of His presence and power, then you are a likely candidate to receive a greater capacity for Him.

Dream-Destiny-Atmosphere Shifters

When you answer the call to a deeper place you become a world changer, a destiny, dream and atmosphere shifter.

Destiny shifters are prophetic people who God uses to literally alter the course or direction of somebody's life by releasing prophetic declarations.

CHAPTER TWO

OVERCOMING YOUR DRY SEASONS

CLOUDS WITH NO RAIN

¹⁴ *Whoso boasteth himself of a false gift is like clouds and wind without rain.* (Proverbs 25:14)

Can you imagine seeing a big, empty, gray and dark cloud overshadowing your entire day, only to discover that in spite of its massive physical appearance, it has no water?

Sadly, this is the case with many people. They are dressed up in all of the religious garb, phylacteries and titles but they have no ability to effect change in someone else's life, or even their own. For the most part, they are void of the true representation of God.

In this hour, God expects every believer to be "pregnant" and filled with prophetic power. He desires that you live up to the expectation of your name and, most of all, to that of His kingdom.

Having "no rain" means that:

- you are spiritually dry
- you are void of the presence and power of God

- you have failed to absorb an anointing from the streams of living water within you
- you have not activated the fruit and gift of the Spirit within you.

Whenever the Spirit of God is absent from your life it is difficult to experience the flow of the anointing.

People whose lives are void of the presence of the Holy Spirit may use their abilities and talents but not their gifting from the Holy Spirit. They sing but the anointing is absent; they may play music but do not have a prophetic flow or impact.

God wants you to have more than just a title or your name on the church roll – He wants you to become a carrier of the glory.

DRY SEASONS

Yes, you may have encountered several breath-taking, life-altering experiences and events which were very dark, inexplicably long and extremely lonely. No doubt, during many of these experiences you were not sure if you were ever coming out of them. These are what I call ***"Dry Seasons!"***

During these times it seems as though nothing is going right in your life and everything you attempt is not successful. You may begin to feel as though you are in a place of drought and barrenness.

If you have been alive long enough you have probably experienced periods in life similar to these ***"Dry Seasons."*** If the truth really be told, you will admit that during your Christian voyage you have had several of them.

Although they may have been intense and arduous, I believe that these are the seasons the Holy Spirit uses to drive you to a place of desiring God more than anything else in the world. It is within these seasons that every desperate seeker finds hope and perfect rest.

A season is considered to be a transitional division of the year marked by distinctive weather conditions. In temperate regions there are four seasons: *Spring, Summer, Autumn and Winter*. On the other hand, in tropical countries there are often only two seasonal shifts – a dry season and a rainy season.

In **Genesis 8:22** God said, "*While the earth remaineth, seedtime and harvest, and cold and heat, and summer and winter and day and night shall not cease.*"

This lets us know that during the course of our lives we would have some hot seasons and cold seasons; we would have some good seasons and, unfortunately some bad seasons.

Although this may be true, **Romans 8:28** reveals that **all** things work together for good for them who love God, even those who are called according to His purpose. For this reason, I believe that even our so-called bad seasons seek to fulfill the purposes of God in our lives.

No matter how many leaves fall off a tree during autumn, and no matter how cold it is during winter, you can rest assured that these leaves will return during spring and summer seasons.

In other words, there will be some seasons when everything around you is going good and then, out of nowhere, something goes very wrong; seemingly outweighing all of your good seasons.

However, the good news is that your bad seasons will not last forever.

OVERCOMING DRY SEASONS

During *"Dry Seasons"* it may seem as if nothing is flowing or growing and, in fact, most people say that these are some of the worst times of their lives.

I remember traveling to minister in a place called *Kakamega, Africa* a few years ago. This area depended heavily on farming but the farmers said that year they experienced one of the worst droughts ever. As a result of their *"Dry Season"* they had very little crop and, therefore, little to no food or money.

During the seven-day revival service, I ministered approximately fourteen times but was reluctant to collect an offering knowing that there was a famine in that area. Nevertheless, I obeyed the Spirit of God and encouraged everyone to find something to sow, no matter what it was. The next day, I saw people walking to the church bringing bunches of bananas, yams and all types of crops – whatever they could gather from their fields.

I was so moved by the love that these people had for God. They did not allow their circumstances to stop them from bringing an offering to the House of God. They decided that with whatever they had they were going to honor God with an offering; even in the midst of a famine.

I do not know what type of **"Dry Season"** you are having right now, whether it is a financial, physical or spiritual one. Please know that God is with you even in the hard times. Even though you may not feel or hear Him, know that He is there. I guarantee you that if you make time for God, then He will make time for you.

As you prepare for your new season, now is the time when you have to gain access to heaven and activate the favor of God over your life. The most significant thing everyone needs in drought is rain. "Rain" or "water" represents the Holy Spirit. Reposition yourself by bearing down in prayer and setting yourself to worship God, regardless of how you may be feeling. You will make it through your dry season.

I have been right there before, with tears running down my face and not knowing where or to whom to turn. These were the nights that I laid in the presence of God just honoring Him and loving Him regardless of how I felt.

Whatever you do, please do not give up. Take courage, find a quiet place to call on the Lord and He will bring you through your **"Dry Season."**

When God begins to turn your dry season into an abundant harvest, please ensure that you do not connect yourself to broken or leaking "cisterns".

BROKEN CISTERNS

The enemy will try anything in his power to stop you from advancing and prospering in the things of God. He will introduce you to various systems which are godless and designed to bring little to no benefit to your life.

These ungodly systems will consume your time, money, talents, abilities and, ultimately, your love for God. These are what I call **"broken cisterns"**.

In **Jeremiah 2:13** the Word of God reveals that, *"...my people have committed two evils; they have forsaken me the fountain of living waters, and hewed them out cisterns, broken cisterns, that* *can hold no water."* You commit two evils whenever you leave the One True God and relinquish your spiritual position.

4 Hear the word of the LORD, O house of Jacob, and all the families of the house of Israel.

5 Thus says the LORD: What wrong did your ancestors find in me that they went far from me, and went after worthless things, and became worthless themselves?

6 They did not say, "Where is the LORD who brought us up from the land of Egypt, who led us in the wilderness, in a land of deserts and pits, in a land of drought and deep darkness, in a land that no one passes through, where no one lives?"

7 I brought you into a plentiful land to eat its fruits and its good things. But when you entered you defiled my land, and made my heritage an abomination.

8 The priests did not say, "Where is the LORD?" Those who handle the law did not know me; the rulers transgressed against me; the prophets prophesied by Baal, and went after things that do not profit.

9 Therefore once more I accuse you, says the LORD, and I accuse your children's children.

10 Cross to the coasts of Cyprus and look, send to Kedar and examine with care; see if there has ever been such a thing.

11 Has a nation changed its gods, even though they are no gods? But my people have changed their glory for something that does not profit.

12 Be appalled, O heavens, at this, be shocked, be utterly desolate, says the LORD,

13 for my people have committed two evils: they have forsaken me, the fountain of living water, and dug out cisterns for themselves, broken cisterns that can hold no water. (Jeremiah 2:4–13)

Reservoirs and "cisterns" are used for holding or carrying water and, if for any reason they become cracked or broken, the water will eventually leak out and be wasted. Likewise, some people who were once deemed as "carriers of the anointing" begin to "leak" issues and valuable "spiritual" resources if they open themselves to erroneous doctrines, fallacies, or seducing spirits.

God never intended His people to go after the things of the world to the detriment of their relationship with Him. However, His desire is that they would seek Him and He would bless them with everything they need.

It is the spirit of the Anti-Christ that resists and rebels against anything that represents God or anything that seeks to advance the Kingdom of God. This spirit seeks to establish its own order, and causes people to align themselves with its ungodly beliefs and worldly systems.

For example, many people have no problem depositing thousands of dollars into a fixed deposit account but will not sow into the kingdom of God. Further, this spirit will make you feel justified in spending hundreds of dollars in the mall on an outfit while giving twenty dollars to God in the offering pan. People generally demonstrate more confidence in worldly systems than they do the kingdom of God.

The enemy has carefully crafted this systematic plan in an effort to draw people away from the One True and Living God while bringing them into bondage and servitude to the dictates of a godless system.

THE SPIRIT OF MARTHA

This is the hour when God is looking for true seekers who will surrender their busy schedules, slow down their pace and cry out to Him. This "surrender" is defined as giving one's will, desires and plans totally over to the mercy of another. In this case it is to give your will, desires, time and attention over to the Almighty God.

It is very difficult trying to speak to someone who is always busy. A "Martha spirit", the spirit of extreme busyness, is seeking to hinder the people of God from getting into His presence. This is a deceptive spirit that has many people operating and functioning in a "good work", even in the house of God, but not settling down long enough to accomplish a "God work."

They have religion but they do not have a relationship with God. They feel more comfortable doing something for Him but not really spending time with Him. In other words they are so consumed with doing every thing that they neglect the most important thing, and that is worshipping at the feet of Jesus.

In **John 6:28–29**, when the disciples asked Jesus what they should do to "work" the works of God, He said that the works of God is to believe in Him. In other words, He was saying that there was nothing in your physical ability that you can use to manifest the presence or power of God in your life, it is an act of the Spirit once you believe.

Therefore, if we are going to have power to fulfill the will of God, we must make the necessary adjustments in our schedules so that we can seek Him. God does not desire to compete with all that is going on in your life; He simply wants to be first.

In order to hear the voice of God you have to posture or position yourself to hear. God wants you to know Him and to know His will for your life. He wants you to be able to discern His voice as opposed to the voice of the enemy and even your own human spirit.

YOU MUST POSITION YOURSELF TO HEAR THE VOICE OF GOD!!!

THE "CARES" OF LIFE

Not experiencing the power of God to the level that you should may be as a result of the fact that you have lost your desire for God. It is not that you do not love God but it is, in part, due to the fact that your desires may now be divided as you confront the daily "cares of life".

Further, this may happen as you try to love and serve God in your new season while you are still locked into an old desire. This is a routine place where you allow all of your issues of life to override your pursuit of God. Your desires become overtaken by the cares of life. For some people it is because of their business, personal goals and aspirations which overshadow their personal, innate pursuit for the presence of God.

When you begin to desire other things more than you desire God, it is not long before God is pushed entirely out of the picture and, seemingly, replaced by other things. For some people it is their career, a desire for a spouse, the desire for wealth, popularity, fame; personal gain; self-attainment and what they are able to accomplish in and of themselves, without God. God is nowhere in the picture and He becomes a faint voice in the ear of those who have moved themselves away from Him. Unfortunately, over a period of time, their lives become void of the power and presence of God.

An interesting point to ponder: *A monk in a monastery who has no spouse or vehicle may be able to hear the voice of God more distinctly and clearly than someone sitting in the highest seat of Silicon Valley, the pinnacle of Wall Street or on the Deacon Board of the church.*

Take time and carefully begin clearing away the clutter in your life as you "cleanse and prepare" you spiritual womb to receive a fresh impartation from the Spirit of God.

CLEANSING YOUR SPIRITUAL WOMB
"Overcoming The Spirit of Barrenness!"

If you find yourself in a spiritually barren or fruitless state, this may be because your spiritual womb has been damaged by scars of hurt, pain, abuse, disappointment, rejection and the like. You may generally have difficulty embracing the things of God and have problems bringing forth anything in the realm of the spirit.

This is, in part, due to the fact that you are still holding on to past disappointments and pain. If you are not careful, you may become a "carrier of pain and disappointment" instead of becoming a carrier of the glory, simply because you have not taken the time to "cleanse" your spiritual womb.

God does not want you to incubate past hurts, disappointments and failures which cause you to remain barren or fruitless. On the contrary, as God seeks intimacy with you, it is His desire to release something in your spirit that will cause you to show forth His glory in the earth realm.

During these precious moments, He will release answers to what you are going through. He will download creative ideas, dreams and visions for your future; solutions to various social ills plaguing your communities and more.

In other words, cleansing your spiritual womb through times of intimate prayer and worship will, through the power of the Holy Spirit, bring intimacy between you and God; ultimately causing you to accomplish great things.

CHAPTER THREE

THE SEEKER'S ANOINTING

BORN TO WORSHIP

I saw something once that was totally amazing to me. Turtles laid their eggs on land but when the eggs hatched, the baby turtles instinctively walked straight towards the water. With no training in swimming, they immediately began to swim.

God created the heavens and the earth, which were initially void and without form. He created the birds to fly, insects to pollinate, fish to swim and the like. He also created the sun, the moon, stars and everything else in this world, and He did so for His glory.

Birds fly, fish swim, flowers bloom, trees grow, lions roar and dogs bark; these are all different expressions of the unique ways in which creation worships and honors God. Likewise, God is calling upon each of us to find our unique identity and worship Him in the manner for which we were created.

"...for I have created him for my glory, I have formed him; yea, I have made him."
(Isaiah 43:7)

In **Isaiah 43:7** God reiterates the fact that He has created man and, more specifically, that man has been created for God's glory. We were born to give God glory; we were born to worship Him. Every human being in this world has an innate desire to worship.

By design, you were created to worship something or someone. Further, God has given every human being a free will and it is His desire that we would choose to worship Him.

In **Acts 19:29–41** the Apostle Paul visits Ephesus and finds several shrines erected. One of them had the inscription, "To the unknown god." The Ephesians were so superstitious that, among the thousands of shrines they had already erected, they built another shrine just in case they forgot to honor one of the gods.

When God created man, the plan was for him to multiply, replenish and subdue the earth and, most of all, to worship and give Him glory. The seed brings forth a plant. A plant begins to bud and bring forth fruit. The fruit is then able to produce a multiple harvest and food that is beneficial to man.

Everything in the world that God created knows its purpose, knows its divine assignment and the reason why it was created.

God wants you to understand your purpose and the reason you were originally created. It is His ultimate desire that you learn and appreciate that your existence has a divine purpose, and that is to worship Him.

He wants us to worship Him to the extent that it separates us and sets us apart from all other creation. He created man to give Him all the glory!

Every day that you wake up should be a day of thanksgiving, a day of praise and a day of glory. God created you in such a way that you have the ability to express worship in your daily lifestyle.

It is important that you come to the revelation that you were created and born to worship God. In Genesis 1 the Bible states that God created man in His own image and likeness. God created man out of the realm of His imagination. In other words, exactly what God thought that man should be is what He created.

Do you understand that you and I were divinely engineered out of the ingenuity and thoughts of God? When God decided to create man He sat down and had a meeting with the Holy Ghost and His Son. He did not merely want to create man like the birds. *(Can you imagine having a beak?)* He did not want to create man to resemble trees but He wanted to create man in His image and in His likeness so that man looks just like Him.

God took great care in the process of creating man in His image and likeness. His ultimate plan was to form and fashion us to act and function like Him. Therefore, when He was finished designing man, He leaned over and breathed Himself–the Ruach of God into man. **(Ruach is a Hebrew word meaning breath of God)**

He breathed His Spirit into man and man became a living soul or *Nephesh which, in Hebrew means living soul.* Man became a spirit speaking being just like God is, was and forever shall be.

This was God's original intent for man. In other words when He breathed His breath into man, man received the ability, authority in the earth realm and the power of God. This may be difficult for many persons to receive, as they believe that by stating this we are placing man on the same level as God. It is imperative for everyone to understand that no man can ever be placed on the same level as God; God is sovereign.

What I am saying here is that man must begin to understand the power, authority and ability that he possesses as a child of God. You cannot casually approach God with your old ways, old mindsets, old attitudes and expect to experience Him in a new way. You cannot come to God with your intellect and expect to understand Him, The Ancient of Days.

Although you may be a believer who loves God and are willing to serve Him, you must begin to "prepare a place" for Him in your life. The Word of God says in **Psalm 22:3** that the Lord inhabits the praises of His people. Your praise creates an atmosphere in which the Spirit of God can dwell. When you praise God, you literally attract His attention and, eventually, His presence, to your life.

A TIME TO SEEK

In **Ecclesiastes 3** the scripture reveals that there is a time, season and purpose for everything under the heaven; a time to weep, mourn, dance, embrace, to make war, to make peace, a time to be born and even a time to die.

As the scripture indicates, there exists a season, time and purpose for everything under the heaven. By definition, **purpose** is the original intent or the reason why something was created; **time** is defined as an instance or occurrence of when something is supposed to happen; while a **season** represents a window of opportunity that you are given, in time, to get something accomplished or achieved.

Therefore, there must come a time in your life when you decide that it is time to seek the Lord. Seek, here, does not merely suggest to look for or to stumble across by happenstance.

Seek, here, means to diligently and intentionally go after something or someone with all of your heart, mind, soul and strength. It means to search out or try to discover; to ask for or to ask of; to go in search of or to earnestly look for. Seek implies a quest or a journey until something or someone is discovered or realized.

Some people go on a quest for worldly knowledge and will spend hours studying a subject until they are well versed on the matter. They seek out relationships with people they are attracted to and will do everything in their power to gain their attention, even if it requires making personal changes or adjustments. For the most part, seeking is born out of one's desperation or desire to have something.

I THIRST FOR MORE

Generally people either seek out what they ardently desire or they go after what they sincerely believe they should have.

In **Psalm 42:1** the Word of God says, **"As the hart panteth after the water brooks, so panteth my soul after thee, O God."**

A deer seeks out water because water is necessary for its existence. If it has no water it will not exist. Therefore, instinctively, water is not an option or a secondary thought, it is a necessity. The deer also knows that it must drink what is necessary to sustain it for its journey through the woods.

In order to be a seeker you must have a burden or passion to pray. This can only come from the Holy Spirit and a balanced lifestyle of cultivating the presence of God. The Word of God states in **Hosea 10:12, "Sow to yourselves in righteousness, reap in mercy; break up** *your fallow ground: for it is time to seek the LORD, till he come and rain righteousness upon you."*

God wants His children to totally, whole-heartedly give themselves up and over to Him seeking to know His divine Will, for His divine Power and to experience His divine Glory. He wants you to desire Him more than you desire anything else in this life. There is a reward for those who make a decision to do so. **Hebrews 11:6** says, "...**he is a rewarder of them that diligently seek Him."**

IT IS THE DESIRE OF THE FATHER THAT YOU SEEK AFTER HIM AS MUCH AS HE IS SEEKING AFTER YOU.

No man can come to the Father except the Holy Spirit draws him. I know that, for the most part, we usually refer to this scripture in reference to salvation, but I believe that it has a deeper meaning.

I believe that every day God is seeking to draw us into His presence. The unction to pray, study His word, worship in your car, share the love of God, give to the work of the kingdom and the like represent times and moments when the Holy Spirit is seeking to draw you closer to God.

GOD WANTS YOU TO DESIRE HIM AS MUCH AS HE DESIRES YOU.

THE SEEKER'S ANOINTING

"It is the glory of God to conceal a thing: but the honor of kings is to search out a matter." (Proverbs 25:2)

The Spirit of God generally does not move in the way that most people anticipate. In His infinite wisdom, God released Jesus to rule as the most powerful king that ever walked the earth. However His humble beginnings of being born in a stable would have never indicated that He had come to complete an assignment of such astronomical proportions.

He released His children out of Egypt and intentionally leads them to a place where they were trapped by their enemies. He called out a king from the house of Jesse and selected David, the least among all of his brethren to be king over the entire nation of Israel. These were all great acts of

God, which He performed in order to display His glory.

Throughout the chronicles of time God has moved however He wanted to move, whenever He wanted and in ways which were beyond human comprehension. Yet he selected a man, Moses, and showed him a supernatural phenomenon through a burning bush that was not being consumed.

In so doing, God was essentially saying is that if He could get Moses' attention long enough He would show Moses greater wonders, such as had never before been seen."

I believe that this is what God is seeking to do with you as you position yourself to seek Him. He will release a greater manifestation of His power and creative ability into your life and, ultimately, your family.

As you intensify your seek He will shift you into a greater dimension of His glory; to a place beyond human reasoning and comprehension; to the realm of God where miracles, signs and wonders are manifesting every day.

The most important thing is that you find God and allow Him to have His way in your life because He wants to use you to do something great.

CULTIVATING THE SEEK

In order for this *"Seek"* to take place there must first be an inner hunger and longing for more of God. This happens cultivating that which has already been deposited inside of you by the Holy 'spirit. As you stir up the gifts within you, your appetite for more of God will increase.

In ***Matthew 5:6*** the Word of God says "...***they which do hunger and thirst after righteousness...shall be filled.***" Each person must see themselves as empty and void, in desperate need of more of God, His presence and power. You must come to realize how incomplete and empty you are without this Great God.

Spiritual cultivation involves preparation and dedicated work through tilling, digging, plowing and nourishment for desired growth. It is taking a scripture and using it as a point of reference, pondering and repeating it until it resonates in our spirit. This is meditation and everyone who walks in the seeker's anointing engages in this practice on a daily basis.

2 "...in His law doth he meditate day and night.

3 And he shall be like a tree planted by the rivers of water, that

bringeth forth his fruit in his season;..."
(Psalm 1:2-3)

WISE MEN CAME FROM FAR

What are you prepared to do in order to be in the presence of God? What is the offering you will bring to honor and celebrate His presence?

10 The reverent and worshipful fear of the Lord is the beginning (the chief and choice part) of Wisdom, and the knowledge of the Holy One is insight and understanding. – Proverbs 9:10 (AMP)

When the wise men sought out Jesus at His birth the already knew that they were on their way to worship a King. They were determined to find Him no matter how long their journey took.

In order to obtain the wisdom of God you must perpetually position your life to discover more about Jesus. If you are building anything in this season without seeking God, you are not wise. Wise men always seek out God first.

***33 But seek ye first the kingdom of God, and His righteousness,
and all these things shall be added unto you." (Matthew 6:33)***

When the wise men found Jesus, they worshipped Him. It did not matter how far they had to travel, they sought Him until they found Him. Once they found Him, they gave Him their best gifts.

THE NICODEUS OF THE NIGHT

In John 3, Nicodemus came to Jesus by night seeking to learn more about Him. He was a ruler in the synagogue of the Jews, but he knew that there was something unique about Jesus and he was determined to find out more. He knew that there was a greater power working in Jesus, one that was outside the laws of Moses. He was familiar with religion but suddenly realized that he did not have a true relationship with God.

I believe that Nicodemus was already saved but was tied to a religious system that had him bound and suffering from a degree of spiritual blindness. Whenever you come to Jesus you must be willing to let go of whatever you are tied to so that you can begin to see, or better, perceive the kingdom of God. *(John 3:3)*

Jesus' instructions to him were that he had to become born again. In other words, Jesus was saying to Nicodemus, "I know you may be saved but your mind needs conversion from religious oppression to total freedom, accepting the kingdom order."

God wants to do something in you beyond anything you have ever experienced. He wants to convert your mind from believing the world system more than you believe Him. He wants you to trust Him more than you trust anything in this world. *You must be born again!*

YOU'VE GOT TO GO DEEPER

Simply attending church on Sunday is not enough. Being saved for numerous years is good, but it is not sufficient. Salvation is only the first step. Your mind must be renewed and rejuvenated.

We are all justified by faith and that faith led you to Jesus. After coming to Jesus you must go through the process of being converted; which means to change the form, character, or function of something. Human flesh and the human mind will never be able to please God. The human spirit, however, is the only thing that can commune with the Spirit of God.

Make a decision to break away and separate yourself from the pleasures of this world. As you do so, you will begin to develop a greater desire for God.

16 For all that is in the world, the lust of the flesh, and the lust of the eyes, and the pride of life, is not of the Father, but is of the world. (1 John 2:16)

CHAPTER FOUR

HEARING THE VOICE OF GOD

SOVEREIGN SPEAKING SPIRIT
"When God Speaks!"

³ *The voice of the Lord is upon the waters; the God of glory thunders; the Lord is upon many [great] waters.*

⁴ *The voice of the Lord is powerful; the voice of the Lord is full of majesty.*

⁵ *The voice of the Lord breaks the cedars; yes, the Lord breaks in pieces the cedars of Lebanon.*

⁶ *He makes them also to skip like a calf; Lebanon and Sirion (Mount Hermon) like a young, wild ox.*

⁷ *The voice of the Lord splits and flashes forth forked lightning.*

⁸ *The voice of the Lord makes the wilderness tremble; the Lord shakes the Wilderness of Kadesh.*

⁹ *The voice of the Lord makes the hinds bring forth their young, and His voice strips bare the forests, while in His temple everyone is saying, Glory!*

10 The Lord sat as King over the deluge; the Lord [still] sits as King [and] forever!

11 The Lord will give [unyielding and impenetrable] strength to His people; the Lord will bless His people with peace. (Psalm 29:3 – 11, AMP)

It has been proven that dogs and other animals tend to hear at a different frequency than human beings. Further, glass has been known to shatter due to the vibration, frequency or pitch of sound to which it is exposed.

The Spirit of God has His own frequency and can only be picked up by those who tune in to His station. I believe that God continues to speak to His people and to anyone who is willing and postures themselves to hear His voice.

It is important to understand that God is a sovereign speaking spirit. In other words, He speaks at a frequency that our human flesh cannot interpret or comprehend. However, as we sharpen our spirit man, we become fully intuitive to His sound.

¹⁴ But the natural man receiveth not the things of the Spirit of God: for they are foolishness unto him: neither can he know them, because they are spiritually discerned. (I Corinthians 2:14)

In **1 Corinthians 2:14** the Word of God reveals that the things of the Spirit of God are foolishness to the carnal man and cannot be understood, because they are spiritually discerned.

However, if your spirit man is active and alive in God then you will be able to hear and interpret the voice of the Spirit. This yieldedness is what causes you to become humbled and broken during times of worship and prayer. The deeper you go and the more you grow in God, He will give you access to understanding and interpreting more of His speaking modes.

THE LORD SPEAKS IN MYSTERIOUS WAYS

God may not always speak to us through an audible voice. However, I believe that there *are a number of ways through which God speaks to us today including, but are not limited to:*

- **Audible Voice Of God** – When God called Samuel, he heard the audible voice of God **(1 Samuel 3:7–10)**

- **Circumstances** – There are times when God allows events to occur in order to give us a message, teach a lesson or demonstrate spiritual truths **(2 Kings 4:1-7)**

- **Utterance Of The Prophet** – The voice of the prophet is generally accepted as the voice of God; prophets convey or reveal the divine will and counsel of the Spirit of God under the mantle of a prophetic anointing **(Isaiah 58:1).** God will do nothing except he reveals it to His servant, the prophet **Amos 3:7**

- **Parables/Allegories** – These are profound earthly stories which have a heavenly meaning **(Matthew 13:18–23)**

- **Through His Word** – God speaks to us distinctly and clearly through His Word (logos) **Hebrews 4:12**; He speaks directly, however, through divine revelation and prophecy (the Rhema word) **Luke 4:18**

- **Miracles** – These are divine interventions of the Spirit of God in the affairs of men **(John 11:32-44)**

- **Interpretive Signs and Wonders**—These are heavenly symbols and representations of the awesome power of God. Healings and other miracles are evidence of this power. **(Exodus 13:21)**

- **Similitudes and Impressions** – These are likenesses, typologies, resemblances or similarities to a person, thing or the like; a likening of one thing that is similar to, or a reflection of, another. For example, Ezekiel in the valley of dry bones. The valley of dry bones is a metaphor God used to describe the spiritual dryness of the house of Israel at that time **(Hosea 12:10)**

- **Types and Shadows** – These are various forms of symbols and demonstrations which tend to represent, demonstrate or explain a spiritual concept. For example, Jonah in the belly of the whale for three days in the Old Testament was a "type" of Christ's burial and resurrection after three days. **(Jonah 1:17; I Corinthians 15:4)**

- **Sounds** and **Vibrations**—A spiritual level of hearing that comes from the realm of the spirit. Spiritual Vibrations or Impressions may manifest in the form of warmth or sensations in one's hands; the ability to discern what God is saying and like occurrences **(1 Kings 18:41; 2 Samuel 5:24)**

- **Dreams & Visions**—God uses "open eye" visions and visions during the night watches in order to inform, warn, instruct or protect His people, especially concerning future events **(Daniel 7; Acts 10–Acts 11).**

HEARING THE VOICE OF GOD

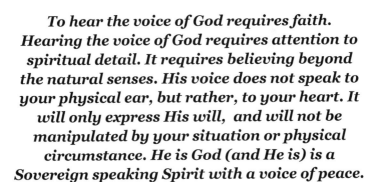

To hear the voice of God requires faith. Hearing the voice of God requires attention to spiritual detail. It requires believing beyond the natural senses. His voice does not speak to your physical ear, but rather, to your heart. It will only express His will, and will not be manipulated by your situation or physical circumstance. He is God (and He is) is a Sovereign speaking Spirit with a voice of peace.

The flesh and carnal man cannot bring Him pleasure. People functioning in the carnal, sensual realm never receive anything from God's speaking voice. Those who, however, take the time to worship, pray and bask before Him will hear truth, instruction and direction for life. – Dr. Mattie Nottage

Hearing the voice of God must become a priority in the life of every believer. I believe that the Spirit of God is speaking to His people. The Word of God says in **John 10:4–5,** *"My sheep know my voice and a stranger they will not follow. . . . . and the sheep follow him, for they know his voice. "*

Spending time in the presence of God will provoke you to follow His voice. Further, He states in **Proverbs 3:6** that if you were to acknowledge Him He would direct your path. Like a Good Shepherd who leads, guides, guards and directs the sheep, God seeks to protect and care for His people.

Therefore, if you are going to progress in the Kingdom of God it is very important and spiritually crucial that you are able to know and hear the voice of God. The Word of God reveals that the Spirit of God will lead and guide us into all truth. It is the Spirit of God that will give you wisdom in your marriage, wisdom in business deals, wisdom for every area of your life; but you can only follow someone's guidance when you are able to hear their instructions.

I believe that there are many people who cannot hear the voice of the Spirit of God, either because they are too busy, distracted or consumed with the "cares of life". Un-busy yourself; God wants to have a conversation with you.

COMMUNICATIONS WITH GOD

The relationship that God desires to have with His people is an intimate one. Similar to every earthly relationship, one of the greatest forms of intimacy begins is communication.

Communication is the exchange of thoughts and ideas through various transmittal forms which may be in the form of verbal or non-verbal; direct or indirect. It is important in every relationship and can be achieved or perceived through tone, emotion, feeling and body language. When communication is conveyed incorrectly or ineffectively it demobilizes, breeds frustration, instigates contention, causes confusion, breeds mistrust and the like.

When we communicate on a personal level, the transmission is a combination of information, thoughts, feelings, intents, desires and more. This exchange may be calm and peaceful or forceful and intense as both individuals engage in the sharing of one's souls.

For the most part, we communicate more intimately with people we know, love, and trust or share a personal relationship. We also tend to communicate freely and vulnerably with people we hold dear to our hearts. The same is true of God.

He will commune or communicate with you as you continue to spend time in prayer and worship. It is God's desire for you to go to a deeper place in Him so that He can fellowship with you in a more intimate way.

PROPHETIC NATAPHS

According to the Strong's Exhaustive Concordance a *"NATAPH"* is a Hebrew word that means to fall in drops, ooze, prophesy or speak by inspiration. The spirit of the Lord releases prophetic sounds through prophetic nataph.

Nataph, sometimes translated "prophet," means "to drop, drip, or distill." It usually includes rain distilling and dripping from the sky, words that "drop" out of someone's mouth, and wine dripping from the mountains in Paradise. It can also be defined as a prophetic drop or droppings from the presence of God.

As we worship the Lord, the Spirit of God takes over our mind and downloads His words, His thoughts and His intents into our spirit. He overtakes our human intellect and our words then become divinely inspired.

In other words, the words that we now speak are no longer uttered as result of our personal knowledge, intellect or human spirit but, instead, by divine inspiration and revelation from God. That one word or prophetic dropping can change someone's entire situation. It is those powerful prophetic Nataph moments that the Spirit of God brings healing and comfort to those in need.

A prophetic nataph is similar sometimes to drops of rain falling. It is a word that God speaks, unexpectedly. It may be in the form of a single word or phrase; a fleeting impression or a snapshot of an image. In whichever form it comes, it is a fleeting moment when, without warning, you know that God has spoken something to you.

In some instances, people may become confused because in seeking answers from God and tend to believe that His most powerful, deepest earth-shattering responses will come in the form of a full paragraph, an entire essay, ten-pages, double-spaced, two thousand words and all. At times He will speak volumes, but there are other times when one word from God can take you on a profound prophetic journey that will forever change your life.

This prophetic journey will include little power nuggets of multi-dimensional revelations of the heart and mind of God. They are gradual prophetic drippings which descend, cascade and, ultimately merge like drops of rain falling from the heavens to culminate in an artistic masterpiece. As the prophet prostrates himself in worship, he begins to receive these droppings from the Holy Spirit.

One drop of heaven's rain can cause a far-reaching ripple effect in the earth realm. Once each portion of the entire revelation has been released, the Holy Spirit then "connects all of the dots" and brings an illumination which radically transforms your life.

You can never get a word, revelation, unction from the Spirit of God and remain the same. One moment in His presence and your life will be forever changed.

The Power of Prophetic Worship

Although the prophetic Nataph in the Hebrew speaks to the might or existence of a prophet, it also embodies the spirit, posture and disposition of the prophetic worshipper.

This profound impartation is borne solely out of prophetic worship and a deeper realm of glory. In other words, you will not partake of this type of experience with God unless you are prepared to enter the realm of God through a deeper realm of worship.

I WANT TO KNOW YOU

Knowing God is entirely different from hearing about God. Knowing God is knowing His character, essence, fragrance, word and will. It is having a keen understanding of who He is and what His divine purpose is in your life.

¹⁰ *That I may know him, and the power of his resurrection, and the fellowship of his sufferings, being made conformable unto his death; (Philippians 3:10)*

It is profound. Paul in my opinion was a great man of God having written over thirteen epistles.

He had experienced the move of God in powerful ways but still wrote and said he wanted to know God better. When you are pressing in to the deeper place, you want to know more and more of God.

In the natural, you would never be transparent or expose yourself to someone who you did not know you or does not know you. Further, you would not share your deepest, most innermost thoughts with someone who you could not trust with the information.

The Word of God reveals in **Psalm 103:7** and **Psalm 25:14** that the Children of God knew the acts of God but Moses knew His ways. It also tells us in Amos 3:7 that God said He would not do anything in the earth realm unless He first reveals it to His prophets. It is referred to as His secret. This lets me know that God sometimes communicates in ways and means which are not obvious or common knowledge to every man.

Moses took time to see God, hear God and know God. It was this relationship of deliberate intimacy by which God knew He could trust him. Therefore, He revealed His greater glory or, better, He revealed His secrets to Moses. I believe that God still loved the Children of Israel but He especially favored Moses because Moses was willing to sacrifice everything he had to get to know Him better.

DISCOVERING THE DIVINE WILL OF GOD

2 It is the glory of God to conceal a thing: but the honour of kings is to search out a matter. (Proverbs 25:2)

According to **Proverbs 25:2** your discovery of the will of God is locked in the epicenter and core of His being. It is hidden deep within the secret chambers of His mind where only you, the seeker, will be able to "dig" and uncover it.

"Divine" signifies something that is God-ordained and established. It is His foremost and utmost thoughts concerning you. Discovering the will of God brings peace, comfort and security. It guarantees success and positions you for glorious victory. It is when we do not know God's will that we are confused and uncomfortable. Once you ask Him for his direction in any matter you position yourself for divine blessings that no enemy can revoke.

11 For I know the thoughts that I think toward you, saith the LORD, thoughts of peace, and not of evil, to give you an expected end. (Jeremiah 29:11)

7 There is a path which no fowl knoweth, and which the vulture's eye hath not seen:

8 The lion's whelps have not trodden it, nor the fierce lion passed by it. (Job 28:7–8)

His divine will is locked in spiritual capsules which are only released in the appointed time and season of your life.   The presentation of your body as a living sacrifice to Him initiates the entire process, unveiling to you exactly what His desires are concerning you.

EMBRACING THE WILL OF GOD

1 I beseech you therefore, brethren, by the mercies of God, that ye present your bodies a living sacrifice, holy, acceptable unto God, which is your reasonable service.

2 And be not conformed to this world: but be ye transformed by the renewing of your mind, that ye may prove what is that good, and acceptable, and perfect, will of God.
(Romans 12:1–2)

Sometimes people mistake the permissive will of God for His divine will. The divine will is exactly what God originally intended and desired for you. His permissive will is what He sometimes allows because of your own personal desires. His divine will is defined as what is good, what is acceptable and what is perfect. It is God's ultimate intention for you regardless of what confronts you. As you present your entire mind, will and emotions to Him, He reveals to you exactly what he wants.

The good, acceptable and perfect will all speak to the divine will of God. It is His one and only true desire concerning you. There are no in-betweens. God is never a God of confusion and chaos; He is a God of comfort and peace.

Throughout the Old Testament God permitted the children of Israel to do some things but this was due to the "hardness of their hearts". As an example, a bill of divorcement was never in the mind of God. The covenant of marriage has always been, and will always be, His plan and ultimate desire for a "love covenant" between a man and a woman. He wanted man to enjoy the pleasures of intimacy in this form; it was never in His plans that a covenant relationship that He had *joined together* would ever be severed.

However, because of man's imperfection and, in some cases, unwillingness to submit to the plan and divine will of God, He instructed Moses to allow the two to separate through a bill of divorcement.

In **Mark 10:2–9** Jesus is dealing with this amended law under the Mosaic Covenant as a rebuke to the Pharisees. Their hearts were not pure toward Jesus and due to their arrogance and pride, they sought to challenge Him with the legality of the bill of divorcement rather than seeking to sincerely understand the heart and mind of God concerning the matter.

2 And the Pharisees came to him, and asked him, Is it lawful for a man to put away his wife? tempting him.

3 And he answered and said unto them, What did Moses command you?

4 And they said, Moses suffered to write a bill of divorcement, and to put her away.

5 And Jesus answered and said unto them, For the hardness of your heart he wrote you this precept.

6 But from the beginning of the creation God made them male and female.

*7 For this cause shall a man leave his father
and mother, and cleave to his wife;*

*8 And they twain shall be one flesh: so then
they are no more twain, but one flesh.*

*9 What therefore God hath joined together,
let not man put asunder.
(Mark 10:2–9).*

Please understand that if you have ever been
divorced for any reason, be it infidelity, neglect or
abuse of any kind (physical, emotional, mental or
otherwise), God does not condemn you.
*There is therefore now no condemnation to
them which are in Christ Jesus, who walk
not after the flesh, but after the Spirit.
(Romans 8:1)*

He says in **Romans 8:1** that there is,
therefore, no condemnation to them who are in
Christ Jesus who seek to walk after the Spirit of
God and not their carnal flesh.

When God said that He hates divorce, what He
was saying is that when He creates a union, it is His
divine will that the two should stay together. Every
marriage ordained by God has a divine purpose and
a specific assignment that He desires to come to

pass. An enduring and endearing marriage is the divine will of God.

I appreciate the Father allowing me to do some things but, if I had a choice, I would prefer to be doing the things that He wants me to do. I firmly believe that in the final analysis, ***"Father knows best!"***

CHAPTER FIVE

NAVIGATING THE REALM OF THE SPIRIT

ENCOUNTERS WITH GOD

¹(To the chief Musician upon Gittith, A Psalm of David.) O LORD our Lord, how excellent is thy name in all the earth! who hast set thy glory above the heavens.

³ When I consider thy heavens, the work of thy fingers, the moon and the stars, which thou hast ordained;

⁴ What is man, that thou art mindful of him? and the son of man, that thou visitest him? (Psalm 8:1, 3–4)

In **John 14** Jesus said, in my Father's house there are many mansions. In this context, a mansion is a realm or a dimension.

In the Kingdom of God there are many realms and dimensions that you can attain. Once you find that place in God, you recognize it as a place of spiritual opulence, power, honor and prestige. These levels, realms and dimensions of revelation, if caught in the realm of the spirit, would position you in a place of profound spiritual consciousness.

The mansion Jesus referred to here is a place prepared and reserved in the realm of God for the true seekers and worshippers. It is specifically for those who desire an audience with The Eternal God and are willing to forever reside in that spiritual place. Spiritual mansions are for people who have passed the test of time, who have overcome adversities and are now wholeheartedly ready to dwell where God dwells in the supernatural realm.

I believe that everyone has an experience with God based on which level of themselves they are willing to offer to God. Man is a triune being comprised of a body, soul and spirit. In this hour God is requiring that those who worship Him must worship Him in spirit and in truth. I believe that those who worship God in spirit are seeking to know Him in a more intimate and deeper way.

I find it interesting that some people can leave a worship experience feeling the presence of the Spirit of God while others claim they got nothing out of the service. I often wondered how some people could leave a service with a healing, deliverance or breakthrough while others leave the same way they came, having received no impartation.

Then the Spirit of God began to show me that at whichever capacity level you seek to approach God, then He will release the same measure of His Spirit to you. If you are only prepared to bring a surface level worship, then He can only release a surface level anointing on your life.

God will never put more on you than you are able and willing to bear. However, if you live a lifestyle of worship and come prepared to worship Him from the depths of your spirit then He will release an abundant measure of His Spirit to you. You will begin finding your way to the Higher Place in God.

ELEVATING IN GOD

Your spirit responds to God. This is the part of man that communes with God. A believer who gives total heart, mind, soul and body to the service of God desires more and more of God every day. They develop a lifestyle of reading the Word, prayer, praise, sowing or giving, meditation, fasting and worshipping God. They seek to cultivate the presence of God wherever they are, whether in their homes, in the grocery store or even at the mall.

In their minds, the presence of God is everywhere and deserves to be worshipped every moment of the day. They seek every opportunity and in every situation to see the manifested presence of God, whether they are in the four walls of the Church or the supermarket. These are the God-seekers. They believe in the power of God which is at work in their everyday lives. They seek opportunities to hear the voice of God. They desire to see everything the way He sees it. They acknowledge God in everything they do; living by the belief that it is truly in Him that they are able to live, move, breathe and have their being. Their every thought is to please Him; body, soul and spirit.

This is the place of hunger and desire to which God wants to draw His people. He likens His presence to our "daily bread"; the air that we breathe; the water after which we thirst...all of these represent things in life which are essential and not secondary.

He wants us to desire Him above every need that we think we have. His desire is to have priority in our lives. The more we go after Him, the more He reveals His glory. It is His desire that we elevate from glory to glory.

NAVIGATING THE REALM OF THE SPIRIT

We live in the earth realm, satan has his kingdom set up in the second dimension, and the throne room or realm of God is established in the third dimension. As we make preparation to enter the realm of God, we must be prepared to transcend the realm of earth, pierce through the realm of darkness and, eventually, penetrate the third dimension.

For the most part, this journey of spiritual navigational involves focused worship and warfare. At times our flesh and other distractions may seek to hinder our ascension through the earthly realm. In other instances, the enemy seeks to launch demonic attacks against us as we are readying ourselves for this spiritual ascension. This ground level or coastal demonic resistance seeks to keep us at the same level in our walk with God while other demonic gatekeepers in our sphere of elevation are set to actively resist our entry to the new spiritual dimension that we are seeking.

As we continue our prophetic ascension we may also begin to encounter more atmospheric interference from territorial and principality demons. At this level the enemy releases spirits of doubt, fear and unbelief to seek to frusrate or hinder your elevation to the third dimension. He does this because he knows that it requires faith to enter the realm of God and the greatest enemies to your faith are fear, doubt and unbelief.

As you intensify our level of prayer, God sends supernatural help and angelic assistance to aid you in navigating and ascending. They wage war against your enemy, clearing a pathway for your movement in the spirit. This is like shifting gears in a car: you start driving in first gear, then shift to second gear. The longer you drive, the more gears you will have to shift into.

Once you are able to intensify and maintain your posture in prayer and worship, then you will defeat these enemies and enter into the realm of God. You will know when you have ascended into the realm of God because you are automatically carried into a prophetic flow.

PROPHETIC STREAMS

Upon entering the prophetic stream your prayer or worship becomes easy; you may lose all track of time, you may lose awareness of your natural surroundings; your appetite is now stimulated for an intimate experience or communion with God; you do not wish to be distracted as you continue to carefully navigate in the realm of the spirit.

While in this prophetic flow you sometimes hear the voice of the Spirit of God. You hear the heart and mind of the Father. He reveals to you new revelations of who He is in this moment of intimate exchange.

As you continue moving in the realm of the spirit you discover that His words may bring you the answers you were searching for; they may give you the encouragement you so badly needed; they may begin to reveal the next plan that He has for you; they may give you wisdom and counsel for something you are facing. His words may also be wise counsel or a revelation for someone else, or something that is happening in your community, city or region. In this realm you are communing with God; it is His moment and He is pouring Himself into you.

THE DEPTH FINDER

Normally, almost every large ship has a depth finder. I am always intrigued by these massive ships, and often wonder how the Captain knows how to navigate the waters to avoid running aground or hitting wreckages, sandbars, and coral or other types of reefs. Then I learned that every big ship has a depth finder.

These **sonar** (**so**und **n**avigation **a**viation and **r**anging) devices are used to estimate the ocean's depth just ahead of the sea path on which the ship is traveling. Navigation involves sea travel, while aviation speaks to air travel.

The depth finder serves several purposes such as helping fishermen to determine: ocean depth and the location of fish, the depth or location of objects in the water and, more importantly, the depth of the water in which these ships must safely navigate. Huge ships without finders are susceptible to fatal accidents and a loss of revenue.

Sound waves are sent down through the waters and bounce back to the sonar device. Once the sound waves hit the ocean floor or an object beneath the water, the distance or rate of speed with which the sound wave travels back to the device helps to determine the water's true depth.

The Holy Spirit on the inside of you is your spiritual depth finder. He releases sound waves in the realm of the spirit to determine our depth in God and to help protect us from impending danger.

If your life is void of the Holy Spirit you stand the risk of becoming a spiritual wreck, possibly destroying or injuring the lives of others, including your own.

Your spiritual depth finder imparts the spiritual gift of discerning of spirits. This provides the ability to recognize spirits and perceive the difference between good and evil, right and wrong, etc. It provides a clear understanding of where you are in God and how to avoid impending danger as you navigate the "seas of life".

Ask the Holy Spirit to guide you and protect you from all danger. Ask Him to reveal to you His divine will and purpose for your life. Once the Holy Spirit is your spiritual sonar device, He will help you to chart a prophetic course in the realm of the Spirit as well as here on earth. He will show you the way that you should go.

CLOUD BY DAY; PILLAR OF FIRE BY NIGHT

If you are going to excel spiritually in the things of God you must, first, have an appreciation for the supernatural power of God. You must have a firm belief and understanding that, because God is Sovereign, He employs His own creative power to perform His mighty acts.

In the book of Exodus, when God used a cloud by day and pillar of fire by night to guide the children of Israel through the wilderness, He was introducing them to a divine **GPS (God's Precise System)** which, to this day, remains unsurpassed.

He allowed an extraordinary cloud to guide them during the day and a bright fiery pillar to blaze a trail that gave them precise directions by night. Whenever you desire more of God He will *"unctionize"* you with the power of the Holy Ghost. It is He, the Holy Ghost, who instructs, teaches, trains and, most of all, guides you into all truth. He becomes your **GPS (God Precise System)** of operation.

SPIRITUAL NAVIGATION

It is interesting to note that just ten years ago having a navigational system in your car was only a dream. Now it would seem as if almost every new car and smart phone comes with one, and it is considered to be a standard feature in each device.

In other words, you do not have to pay additional monies to own one. The factory manufactures a device that is tailor-made to the make and model of your car. The deeper you go in the Spirit of God the easier it becomes to navigate and find your way in the things of God. The more of God's presence you seek, the easier it is for you to know the mind and will of God in every situation.

Things that you were once blind and oblivious to now become clearer. You no longer find yourself hindered, at dead ends but, rather, you now find yourself on clear pathways pointing you in the specific direction that God has predestined for you. You now possess the spiritual MapQuest.

SPIRITUAL MAPQUEST

I recently recounted to my kids an experience I had when I arrived two hours late to my doctor's appointment. The drive, according to them, should have only taken fifteen minutes. They stood in utter amazement and waited for me to explain, verbatim, what had happened.

My driver at the time had emphatically assured me that we were only fifteen minutes away from the address we had been given, and insisted that we stop and have a light lunch since there was no traffic to delay us.

I asked if she was certain about this and suggested that we *"MapQuest"* the directions before we went to lunch. Again, she insisted that she was familiar with the area and would have me at my appointment well within the scheduled time.

We sat down, ate leisurely and thoroughly enjoyed our meal, then casually headed on our way. Unfortunately, however, when we arrived at the intended address, it was not the correct location. After we eventually MapQuested the directions, we discovered that we were over forty-five minutes away. By this time, School had already been dismissed and the "School Zone" speeds enforced. We never got to the appointment until two hours later.

Needless to say, I was not very happy about the entire ordeal. If my driver had simply taken two minutes to MapQuest the directions as I had suggested, this would have saved us two hours of unnecessary tardiness.

In **Proverbs 3:6** we are advised to acknowledge God in **all** our ways then He will direct our path. God does not want you to miss any divine appointments with Him. Take a moment before you make any decision in life, no matter how big or small, and consult God.

Ask Him quietly what is His will concerning the matter. Ask Him what He wants you to do and what is His will concerning you. He always answers. He knows your destiny and the route you should take to get there.

DIVINE SPIRITUAL SURVEILLANCE
"Tracking And Tracing God!"

Most shipping companies use a tracking or tracing system to provide their customers with the facility of determining where their package is during transshipment. This, no doubt, provides comfort and peace of mind to the customer, although they have not received their physical package.

They know its whereabouts and, more importantly, that it is on the way. God wants you to develop your spiritual tracking system so that locating Him is not difficult or arduous, especially during the time of trouble or distress. *(Psalm 27:1-6)*

Most people wait until tragedy strikes or they have a 9-1-1 emergency before they attempt to locate God. They spend little to no time in prayer, learning how to connect with Him. Unfortunately, more often than not they ignore His voice prior to their dilemma, finding it difficult to trust Him for their total breakthrough and ultimate victory.

You should know that a fully developed and charged spirit that senses God will know exactly where to find Him, especially in the time of trouble. Better yet, God will know where to find you during your time of despair or whenever you greatly need Him. Moreover, He will know exactly where to find you to release your blessings to you.

Care must be taken to intentionally and consistently spend time developing and sharpening your surveillance tracking system for your overall success in life and spiritual wellbeing.

Take time to activate the gifs of the spirit, especially the revelatory gifts of discernment of spirits, the spirit of The Word of Wisdom, and the spirit of the Word of Knowledge.

PROPHETIC DIRECTION

Being filled with the Holy Ghost provides prophetic direction in all things. This does not mean that you will not make a mistake or take a wrong turn. It simply means that if you do take a wrong turn, the Spirit of God will point you in the right direction.

13 There hath no temptation taken you but such as is common to man: but God is faithful, who will not suffer you to be tempted above that ye are able; but will with the temptation also make a way to escape, that ye may be able to bear it.
1 Corinthians 10:13

CHAPTER SIX

ON MOUNTAINS SO HIGH

"I Still Want You!"

MOUNTAINTOP JESUS VERSUS TABLE-TURNING JESUS

God desires to take you to a high place in Him. Isaiah speaks of Him being the God of the valleys and the God of the mountains. In other words, He is omnipresent and dwells everywhere. The valleys are designed for preparation while the mountains are for elevation. Every seeker should strive to have mountaintop experiences in Him.

In **Matthew 21**, the Bible gives an account of the fanfare that Jesus received as He entered the city of Jerusalem. Many removed their garments and laid them before Him as He rode through the streets on a donkey that had been reserved for this specific occasion.

Many sang His praises and gave glory to God saying, "Blessed is He who comes in the name of the Lord!" It was clear that the people had been greatly blessed by His ministry and were celebrating the One who they had deemed their Savior. The Bible even speaks about how this regal, triumphal display had greatly impacted the entire city.

However, just a few short verses later the Bible also records that Jesus enters the Temple, His Father's house, and became grieved by what He saw. The holy Temple of God which was originally consecrated as a place for the people of God to worship and pray had been converted into a corrupted, ungodly marketplace. People no doubt were being defrauded, moneychangers given to usury, while doves and other animals for sacrifice were being bought and sold.

In **John 2:14–16** the Bible records how Jesus plaited a whip and used it to drive them all out of the Temple as He quoted from **Isaiah 56:7** that the House of God is a House of Prayer. However, their carnal, religious mindsets had demeaned it by making it into a "den of thieves".

Many of the people became offended because Jesus had destroyed their businesses, interrupted their program and drove them out of the temple. They had soon forgotten that just a few short moments before that they had celebrated and embraced Him as their king.

After such a sharp rebuke, would you be able to say, *"I Still Want You, Lord?"* Would you still be in the congregation of those singing, *"Hosanna, Blessed is He who comes in the name of the Lord",* or would you turn away from Him, offended that He had interfered with your religious rituals or done something that you did not agree with? *(John 6:66)*

Do You Still Want Him?

On your journey of spiritual acquisition and attainment embrace Him in whichever form He comes. Many people are willing to seek after the "Mountaintop Jesus" who speaks profound revelations of a glorified kingdom but few, however, are willing to embrace the "Table-turning Jesus" who rebukes them sharply as He seeks to correct their wrong.

The once popular Jesus, who raised the dead, cast out demons, laid hands on the sick and made them recover, is now labeled as a *table-turner*. Now you have to decide: do you only want the table-turning Jesus or do you only want the "Mountaintop" Jesus? Can you sincerely say that no matter how Jesus reveals Himself, you still want Him?

"Want" comes out of the emotional realm of your soul and speaks of your desires or what you long for. If you can continue to desire Him, He will come and fill the desires of your heart.

After every experience with Jesus, whether on the mountaintop or turning tables, we must be willing to embrace Him, even if there is a price to pay.

PROPHETIC ASCENSION
"Navigating His Presence!"

Over the years, I have experienced various depths and heights in God. From the natural realm it would appear that these experiences vacillated between very low or obscure places and, alternately, realms of glory.

There were seasons, though, where I felt like my life was going in complete circles and, sometimes, even spiraling out of control. However, during the periods of obscurity, I was often drawn to seek the Lord because since childhood I knew that there was safety in His presence.

As I spent more and more time navigating the realm of the Spirit I began to understand that although there were times of uncertainty and confusion, my low places were not just seasons of digression in my walk with God but, through the realm of prophetic insight, the Spirit of the Lord began to show me that I was experiencing what are called levels of **prophetic ascension**.

3 Who shall ascend into the hill of the LORD? or who shall stand in his holy place? (Psalm 24:3)

Although in my mind it seemed like I was losing ground in the realm of the Spirit, the Holy Spirit began to show me that what was actually happening was, although I found myself at a low place, it was in a higher dimension. He further revealed to me that the low place was necessary in that it prepared and trained me for the time when I would be elevated to the high place within that dimension.

He told me that whatever I did in my low place would affect what happens when I elevated to the mountaintop. In other words, my attitude and spiritual disposition during my "valley" or low experiences would help to determine my spiritual disposition on the mountaintop. If you come out of your "valley" experiences fearful and uncertain, then you will approach you mountains with the same attitude.

Further, this mode of prophetic ascension would perpetually include cycles of highs and lows which would pattern the way that I would elevate to higher and higher dimensions.

THE GOD OF THE MOUNTAIN

We typically say that God is the God of the mountain and the God of the valley. This simply means that no matter what state you find yourself in, God will still be God in your life. Further, as you continue to mature in the things of God, you will begin to understand more and more that both the "mountaintop" and "valley" experiences serve their own specific purposes.

Your "mountaintop" experiences are realms of power or glorified places in your life. On the other hand, your "valley" experiences are difficult, challenging encounter; designed to prepare you for the glory that God will reveal in a specific season in your life.

Throughout the scriptures, God generally performed many of His most profound works on a mountaintop. The human agents, through which He operated all rendered some level of sacrifice in order for this glory to be revealed.

**SOME OF THESE GOD ENCOUNTERS
INCLUDED BUT ARE NOT LIMITED TO:**

Mount Carmel   **Mount Sinai**
Mount Moriah   **Mount Calvary**

MOUNT CARMEL
(The Glory on Mt. Carmel)

1 Kings 18:36-38

36 And it came to pass at the time of the offering of the evening sacrifice, that Elijah the prophet came near, and said, Lord God of Abraham, Isaac, and of Israel, let it be known this day that thou art God in Israel, and that I am thy servant, and that I have done all these things at thy word.

37 Hear me, O Lord, hear me, that this people may know that thou art the Lord God, and that thou hast turned their heart back again.

38 Then the fire of the Lord fell, and consumed the burnt sacrifice, and the wood, and the stones, and the dust, and licked up the water that was in the trench.

MOUNT CARMEL
"The Place of Confrontation"

On Mount Carmel, God will release supernatural power for you to confront every principality challenging your life. He will seek to have you rise up in prophetic power and defeat every spirit of Jezebel.

MOUNT MORIAH
(The Glory on Mt. Moriah)

Genesis 22:2
And he said, take now thy son, thine only son Isaac, whom thou lovest, and get thee into the land of Moriah; and offer him there for a burnt offering upon one of the mountains which I will tell thee of.

2 Chronicles 7:1-2
1 Now when Solomon had made an end of praying, the fire came down from heaven, and consumed the burnt offering and the sacrifices; and the glory of the LORD filled the house.

2 And the priests could not enter into the house of the LORD, because the glory of the LORD had filled the LORD's house.

MOUNT MORIAH
"The Place of The Ultimate Sacrifice!"

On Mount Moriah, Abraham was willing to give God the ultimate sacrifice, his son. At this Mount of glory, God requires of you a noble sacrifice and, in some cases, the ultimate sacrifice.

MOUNT SINAI
(The Glory On Mount Sinai)

Exodus 19:18

And Mount Sinai was altogether on a smoke, because the Lord descended upon it in fire: and the smoke thereof ascended as the smoke of a furnace, and the whole mount quaked greatly.

Exodus 31:18 - And he gave unto Moses, when he had made an end of communing with him upon Mount **Sinai**, two tables of testimony, tables of stone, written with the finger of God.

MOUNT SINAI
"The Place of The Ultimate Sacrifice!"

Mount Sinai, the Spirit of the Lord descended in the likeness of a dark cloud. This signifies that, in the midst of every dark situation, God will still speak and show Himself as God. He will give you new directives and instructions which will seek to govern your life.

MOUNT CALVARY
(The Glory On Mount Calvary)

Luke 23:44–46

44 And it was about the sixth hour, and there was a darkness over all the earth until the ninth hour.

45 And the sun was darkened, and the veil of the temple was rent in the midst

46 And when Jesus had cried with a loud voice, he said, Father, into thy hands I commend my spirit: and having said thus, he gave up the ghost.

MOUNT CALVARY
"The Place of The Ultimate Sacrifice!"

Mount Calvary represents a place of total surrender and sacrifice. This is a place of reference to activate the power of the blood of Jesus to work in your life.

WORSHIP + SACRIFICE = GLORY

THE RETURN OF THE GLORY OF GOD

In order to experience levels and realms of God's glory and to maintain His glory in your life you must:

- become broken and yielded
- be willing to die to "self" or selfish desires
- be willing to sacrifice.

The Bible speaks of David being a man after God's own heart. Although he was one of the greatest kings of Israel, David was also a worshipper. He knew how to wield a sword, slay giants and defeat the armies of the enemies of Israel. Yet he also knew how to lay prostrate in the presence of the One he esteemed as the King of all kings, in brokenness and humility.

David was not perfect and did not always do everything right, but he always knew how to find a place of repentance that moved the heart and hand of God in his favor. *(Psalm 51)*

God's Due Order

"...the Lord our God made a breach upon us, for that we sought him not after the due order." (1 Chronicles 15:13)

When the Ark of the Covenant had been stolen by the Philistines King David decided to bring the Ark back to the house of Israel.

Although his intentions were pure and he sincerely wanted to please God, he sought to return the Ark on a new cart, which was not what God wanted. God's original intention was that the priests would carry the Ark because He always meant for His people to be carriers of the glory. *(1 Chronicles 15)*

GLORY CARRIERS

God wants you to become a glory carrier. He desires that we continuously increase our capacity for the Spirit of God by living a lifestyle of prayer, worship, fasting and studying His Word.

He has a precise order in which He desires you to operate. He is requiring that everything around you comes into divine alignment with His will for your life in order for the glory of the Lord to be revealed to, and through, you.

CHAPTER SEVEN

THE CLARION CALL TO WORSHIP

DISCERNING THE SOUND
"The Clarion Call To Worship!"

Growing up on a small island, every Sunday morning the church bell would ring throughout our neighbourhood. You could hear the big bell ringing very loudly for many miles. It was an alarm to awake everyone, announcing that it was time for prayer and Sunday morning worship. God is now releasing a new sound in the earth. It is a clarion call to wake up and seek Him

Sound creates movement in the realm of the Spirit. This is why in John 6:63 Jesus says the words that I speak are spirit and life. Just as Jesus was able to actívate movment in the realm of the spirit by speaking the Word, you have that same ability to do so.

And Jesus said unto them, Because of your unbelief: for verily I say unto you, If ye have faith as a grain of mustard seed, ye shall say unto this mountain, Remove hence to yonder place; and it shall remove; and nothing shall be impossible unto you. (Matthew 17:20)

This is why he says in **Matthew 17:20** that if you speak to the mountain and tell it to be removed that it will move. If you could build your faith to the degree where you understand that nothing is imposible to you, if you would only speak it in faith.

The Dynamics of Sound

Sound creates movement in the realm of the spirit. This is why in *John 6:63* Jesus says the words that I speak are spirit and life. You have that same ability to speak or declare a thing and watch it come to pass. The spoken word is a spiritual activator; you will have whatsoever you say. *(Mark 11:24)*

For the most part, every move of God is predicated with a specific *sound* or *song*. This sound announces a shift in the prophetic atmosphere and reveals the purpose of God in that season.

Sound has typically been defined as a wave or disturbance that is created by vibrating objects and is transmitted through various mediums. Sound can be transmitted through the air, through water or some other physical device.

A sound can be transported either by moving along a wave traveling in the same direction or it can be generated by one particle hitting against another. Further, sound is usually measured in units called **decibels.**

The faintest sound that the human ear can detect is called the **threshold of hearing**. At this level sound can be measured at 1×10^{-12} Watts per square meter. The most intense sound that the human ear can withstand without being damaged is 1×10^{-3} Watts per square meter, one billion times more intense than the threshold of hearing.

Sound waves can also be transmitted with varying levels of intensity and power. It has been said that the greater the height of the sound wave, the louder or more intense the sound.

The Spirit of God is constantly releasing sounds and utterances from heaven at certain frequencies. If you are going to hear His voice you have to cultivate an atmosphere in which you can detect this frequency.

Sound and vibration travel in waves. The vibration in the Spirit realm helps you to interpret the sound of the Spirit. The vibration is an indication that the Spirit of God is speaking.

DEMONIC SOUND BARRIERS

As a result of our fast-paced, modern society many are spending less and less time in the presence of God and are, thus, becoming insensitive to His voice. If you are going to hear anything from the Spirit of God, you must make an effort to posture yourself to hear His voice.

In the Garden of Eden, when Adam moved himself away from the Spirit of God he could no longer hear the voice of God, and, when he did hear the voice of God, he became anxious and afraid. In other words, he lost his place of spiritual authority and confidence in God. Similarly, when we can no longer hear the voice of God we may become confused and spiritually demobilized.

I believe that the enemy seeks every opportunity to release demonic sound barriers, such as deaf and dumb spirits, in order to obstruct or distort the sound that is coming from the presence of God.

This demonic sound barrier is designed to cause the believer to become void of hearing the voice of the Spirit of God and more prone to hearing the voice of man or the world. This happens when we, as the people of God draw ourselves away from the presence of God.

THE REALM OF GOD

In the spirit realm there are levels, realms and dimensions which God has ordained for us to aspire to in life.

A **realm** is a place, a sphere, a domain, a region, a kingdom. A **dimension** is a higher level of thought; there are a number of different realms that exist, some of which are:

- **The earth realm** where mankind and other living creatures dwell
- **The spiritual realm** comprises of two opposing realms, the realm of God and the realm of satan
  - **The supernatural Kingdom of Heaven and the realm of God** where God and His angels dwell
  - **The satanic realm** where satan and his demons dwell.

God is trying to take us into a higher place or realm of thinking, believing or operating. This place is called "the realm of God."

- There is no fear, doubt or unbelief here.
- There is no failure here.
- This is a place of trusting.
- This is a place of existing that will bring heaven to earth right where you are.

The only way to attain these levels is if we remain in **divine alignment** with God where a person lines up or positions himself to remain in agreement with the movement of the Spirit of God.

In order to experience the fullest measure of the glory of God in your life, He has to divinely connect you with the right people, places, vision, etc.

The **Realm of God** is a place where God dwells; this is a realm of the supernatural; a realm where all things are possible. It is a spiritual place that you attain unto as you begin to worship God.

THE SECRET PLACE

He that dwelleth in the secret place of the most High shall abide under the shadow of the Almighty (Psalm 91:1)

The deeper place in God is synonymous to the secret place referenced in **Psalm 91**. In this place, you are "hidden" and protected from the plots, plans and schemes of the enemy. In the secret place you are beyond demonic radars of hurt, abuse, rejection, neglect, worry, fear and the like. The enemy cannot "find" you or "calculate" your demise. This is a place God has prepared so that He can commune with you.

He draws you into the secret place so that He can deposit something in your spirit. Here is where the intimacy you share is most intense. He desires to commune with you, uninterrupted, untimed....in the secret place. In this place the worship experience propels you to a higher dimension; all of your doubts and fears are dispelled in the secret place.

The first thing you must understand is that God does not always give you full details on where this place is located. However, you can always tell when you have been called to the Secret Place. Even though there are a lot of details, there are always precise instructions. He will sometimes give you minute instructions which require your obedience.

In obeying these instructions, the way to the Secret Place will begin to unfold before you. It is a divine pathway that leads you on a profound journey to the secret place. Every seeker must be prepared to and determined to find it.

"...straight is the gate and narrow is the way, which leadeth unto life, and few there be that find it" (Matthew 7:14)

The way to the Secret Place is very straight and extremely narrow. It is a tight walk that only a few people are willing to take because it requires much sacrifice. I have discovered that many people never find the secret place of God because of demonic distractions. Satan uses various tactics in the form of tragedy, family crisis, sickness, disappointment and other cares of life to subvert you from ever finding this place in God.

For example, when you feel a desire to pray he conveniently causes unexpected situations such as your phone ringing, your children becoming unusually unruly or someone disturbing you with frivolous matters that could have waited or you may begin to experience unexplainable disagreements with your spouse.

The reason why the enemy causes such disturbances in your spiritual atmosphere is because he (the devil) has been to the Secret Place before. He already knows the infinite power that exists in the presence of Almighty God, so it is his personal mission to prevent you from ever entering that deeper place. In other words he already has an idea what will be bestowed upon you once you enter the Secret Place of God.

It will be a fight, and you must decide to fight regardless of the warfare before you. There will always be intense warfare before prophetic ascension and spiritual elevation.

Jesus made it very clear that if anyone was going to follow Him, they must be willing to first:

- Deny themselves
- Take up their cross
- And then follow Him

Unfortunately, most people today take up a calling but have not taken up their cross to follow Jesus. They opt to enjoy the glitz and glamour of ministry rather than making the necessary preparation to be effective in ministry.

How To Enter The Secret Place

To enter the Secret Place you must determine that you are going to press your way in, beyond the plots and plans of the enemy, beyond the opinions of others and beyond your own personal inhibitions. You must be willing to take drastic and deliberate measures to enter into the presence of God.

Whenever "the water" of the Holy Spirit is stirred in you and you feel an urge compelling you to come into His presence, readily embrace that moment. Posture yourself before Him, pouring out your soul in broken worship; releasing yourself totally over to the Hoy Spirit of God. Allow Him to overtake and overshadow you with His power.

When you have broken forth beyond all of the distractions and find yourself in a place of total surrender, unable to control yourself or physically contain what is happening to you, then you know that you have entered the Secret Place. Nothing in the natural realm matters anymore, not even time.

Now That You Are There

Now that you are there nothing else in the whole world matters. It is just you and God, the One you came seeking. It is your spiritual paradise; a place of total bliss. It is so profound that words can barely describe the surreal encounter you are now having.

You want the experience to last forever, so you bask and wait to hear if only one whisper from the Sovereign King to soar with Him. Your life is never the same again and everyone will know it.

RESEVOIRS FOR HIS GLORY

I believe that God created everything in the natural as a physical representation of what occurs in the realm of the spirit. Throughout the scriptures, the Holy Spirit has been likened or referenced to as various phenomena.

He has been described as a dove at Jesus' baptism, a mighty rushing wind and cloven tongues of fire as on the day of Pentecost. The Holy Spirit has also been likened to water flowing. It is the desire of the Spirit of God that we become reservoirs for His presence.

> *37 "...Jesus stood and cried, saying, If any man thirst, let him come unto me, and drink.*
>
> *38 He that believeth on me, as the scripture hath said, out of his belly shall flow rivers of living water.*
>
> *39 (But this spake he of the Spirit, which they that believe on him should receive:..." (John 7:37–39)*

Water represents the movement and presence of the Holy Spirit. Bodies of water can be represented in various forms. Symbolically, the size of each body of water can represent the level or magnitude of the movement and presence of the Holy Spirit in your life as a believer.

Bodies of water are defined as a significant gathering of water in one defined area. Therefore, a small body of water can be identified as a puddle, wetland or stream, while larger bodies of water can represent lakes, rivers, oceans and seas.

- **Puddles, also known as ripples** are some of the smallest bodies of stagnant water which generally form after it rains. These bodies of water spawn and grow tadpoles, mosquitoes and other such insects. Ripples or slight stirrings can be formed in this body of water from other drops of water.

 SPIRITUAL PUDDLES – This body of water represents someone who is spiritually non-productive and void of the presence of God. Because of the lack of water flow this person is susceptible to spiritual contaminants and other maladies. God is calling

believers to move from this realm of anointing.

■ **Streams are considered to be small flowing bodies of water.** Although streams flow, they are slow moving and generally run in one specific direction. Typically, streams tend to flow within a contained area or region as they converge with the more powerful currents of a river.

SPIRITUAL STREAMS – This body of water represents someone who is spiritually operating in a "surface" level anointing. This is the person who remains content with just coming to Church and connecting with the spiritual climate there without seeking to cultivate the presence of God for themselves. These people are "Conference" or "Prophecy" Junkies who live their lives waiting for the next prophecy or Revival without seeking to activate the Word that God has already spoken in their lives. God wants His people to begin to mature beyond this level of faith.

- **Lakes – Lakes are bodies of fresh water which do not flow.** It is contained or surrounded by land and does not flow into a larger ocean or sea. Some lakes are man-made whereas others are natural. Lakes are generally used for recreation and small scale irrigation. The largest lake in the world is Lake Superior, which is found in North America. This massive lake measures 31,698 square miles with an average depth of 500 feet.

- **SPIRITUAL LAKES – This body of water represents a believer who spiritually satisfied knowing the Word of God but who has not intentions of growing or expanding in the things of God. This person is content with reading their Bible and occasionally sharing their faith with others. If not careful, this person can become very religious and void of a true, intimate relationship with God. God is calling His people out of this level of mediocrity and complacency into a deeper place in Him.**

- **Rivers – Rivers are larger streams of fresh water flow** which are formed by the convergence of streams or other smaller bodies of water. Rivers are vaster than streams or lakes and have a more powerful flow or current. The size of a river is generally calculated based on where it originated from or its source to the mouth of the river, the point just before it connects to an ocean or sea. This source generally originates from elevated land masses, hills, mountains and the like. The passage through which the river flows is called the river's bed. The land masses on each side of the river are called the river's banks. Rivers tend to flow through multiple countries, impacting the geographical and economic landscape of an entire region. The longest river in the world is the River Nile which is 4,132 miles long, flows at a rate of 5,180 m^3 per second and eventually joins into the Mediterranean Sea. Typically, rivers were used for irrigation, commerce, industry, transportation, etc.

SPIRITUAL RIVERS: In this spiritual realm, the believer is experiencing greater levels of the power of God in his life. At this level he is able to discern the realm of the Spirit more so than another believer who is living

at a "lake-like" faith level. In this realm, the believer understands that God is his source and is able to tap into His presence. Further, he possesses a level of understanding, discernment and spiritual insight into the things of God. This person's influence is also able to extend beyond his own immediate environment, personal sphere of influence, and community as he connects with others who possess the same or greater level of the presence of the Spirit of God.

Oceans and Seas – It is estimated that seventy-five percent (75%) of the entire earth is covered with water. These waters have further been classified as oceans or seas. By definition, there has been a longstanding discussion among various oceanographers as to the distinction between oceans and seas. Both are defined as massive bodies of water. However, for the most part, a sea is considered to be a large or massive body of water surrounded by continents. Further, The Sea, as defined with a definite article is the collective term used to refer to all of the oceans of the earth such as the Pacific, Atlantic, Indian, Southern and Arctic Oceans.

SPIRITUAL OCEANS AND SEAS: These bodies of water represent an abundance of the presence of God. This is a spiritual place of no-end, or limit, in God. It is a place where you have to trust God; a place where anything is possible and where you experience the presence of God like you have never experienced it before. Spiritual floods and tsunamis are created in this depth. This realm of the spirit represents a place where carnal people will not come; a place beyond this world's system and their own selfish desires. It is a spiritual realm where the believer desires more of God and seeks to connect with others who are seeking a deeper place. These are the glory seekers who desire to experience the limitless realm of God.

In ***Genesis 1:2 "The Spirit of God hovered over the face of the deep ...."*** This movement upon the face of the water is symbolic of the fact that the Spirit of God has been seeking to prepare the earth for a great outpouring of His power. It represents the stirring that is taking place, even now, in the realm of the spirit.

In this hour, God is looking for those who are in search of a greater outpouring of His Spirit. However, if you are truly seeking a deeper walk with God, you will never find Him lurking in shallow waters or on the banks of spiritual rivers. He is always found in the deeper place.

SPIRITUAL OR PROPHETIC GEYSERS

Dew, mist, rain, snow, waterfalls, geysers and other water forms in the natural realm all have spiritual implication or symbolism.

A geyser is a spring of water that is characterized by the random, forceful emission of hot water and steam. This period emission of water and steam can reach heights of over 300 feet.

Sporadic eruptions occur as the water in the geyser flows to the earth's heated surface through various pockets in the earth. Once the water heats and begins to boil, it gushes forth out of the geyser reaching hundreds of feet in the air.

As it is in the natural so it is in the spirit. I believe that God is speaking to His people and there will be those who embrace His word and will respond to Him like a spiritual or prophetic geyser. For example, people who suddenly feel the presence of God may react with a brief shout while others may literally "break off running" as a result of the power of the Holy Spirit.

THE PROPHETIC FLOW OF THE SPIRIT

8 And The LORD God Planted A Garden Eastward In Eden; And There He Put The Man Whom He Had Formed.

9 And Out Of The Ground Made The LORD God To Grow Every Tree That Is Pleasant To The Sight, And Good For Food; The Tree Of Life Also In The Midst Of The Garden, And The Tree Of Knowledge Of Good And Evil.

10 And A River Went Out Of Eden To Water The Garden; And From Thence It Was Parted, And Became Into Four Heads.

The Bible records in **Genesis 2:10**, that this one river from the Garden of Eden burst into four major streams of increase.

I believe that these streams of increase which are getting ready to flood the earth include, but are not limited to:

- Revelation and understanding of the Word of God
- Cultivation and demonstration of the Fruit of the Spirit
- Divine activation and release of the gifts of the spirit, which include miracles, signs and wonders
- Creative wisdom to execute business; to obtain wealth and prosperity in the market place

I also believe the nature and characteristics of each stream reveals the manner of the prophetic flow of the Spirit of God through these médiums. I further believe that God will begin to demonstrate His power in ways we have never seen before.

9 But as it is written, Eye hath not seen, nor ear heard, neither have entered into the heart of man, the things which God hath prepared for them that love him.
(1 Corinthians 2:9)

THE RIVERS OF EDEN

As we begin to tap in to the resevoir of God, God is going to cause the Church to burst forth into four streams:

1) THE RIVER PISON
- To Increase
- To Spread
- To Grow Fat
- To Expand/Expansion
- To Exponentially Increase; to grow without measure
- To exceed or go beyond the natural ability to calculate

God is going to bless and increase you. Whatever you have sown, God will supernaturally multiply and increase it beyond measure. He will take your "seed", multiply it and give you a harvest. *(Matthew 13:8)*

Therefore, this prophetic release will be poured out:
- **Some 30 Fold** where He is adding to you
- **Some 60 Fold** where He is multiplying you blessings
- **Some 100 Fold** where He is increasing you exponentially

2) THE GIHON RIVER

- Bursting Forth
- To Come Forth
- To Make Happen
- To Posses
- To Take
- To Acquire
- To Birth Forth

God is releasing a treading anointing upon His people to acquire new territories and dimensions in the realm of the spirit. He is requiring His people to lengthen their cords and strengthen their stakes in order to grow, expand and possess new opportunities. *(Isaiah 54:2; Psalm 18:33)*

3) HIDDEKEL RIVER

- Rapid or quick
- Swift like a gushing river
- to issue forth suddenly and forcibly
- to be extremely full
- to appear suddenly

In *Isaiah 43:18–19* the Word of God reveals that God is ready to do a new thing in your life and it is His desire that it would spring forth speedily.

4) THE RIVER EUPHRATES

- Fruitful
- Productive
- Successful
- Abundant
- Profitable

- Rewarding
- Bountiful
- Over Abundant
- Inexhaustible

The Word of God says in **Hebrews 11:6** that God is a rewarder of them that will diligently seek Him. It is His desire to release a blessing in your life that is exceeding and abundantly above all that you could ever ask, think or image. *(Ephesians 3:20)*

PROPHETIC WORD: THE GLORY OF GOD

This is what the Lord Almighty says in the book of Haggai: "In a little while I will once more shake the heavens and the earth, the seas and the dry land.

There is about to be a spiritual earthquake. This shaking has to do with a Pentecostal experience like as the day of Pentecost; like rushing mighty winds which shook the house, earthquakes which bring revival and restoration. (Ezekiel 37)

Paul and Silas were locked in prison and, as they released a praise, this evoked an earthquake so strong that it shook the prison bars open and allowed them to go free.

I will shake all nations, and the desires of all nations will come, and I will fill this house with glory," says the Lord Almighty.

Those nations that have been in travail shall see the glory of the Lord revealed and manifested. The return of the full demonstration of the power of God will cause a release of silver, gold and wealth. "The silver is mine and the gold is mine," declares the Lord Almighty.

"The glory of this present house will be greater than that of the former house," says the Lord Almighty. "And in this place I will grant peace," declares the Lord Almighty." (Haggai 2:9)

This is what Haggai is referring to—God coming and taking charge. When Kabod comes, God is present with us. God is taking charge. When Kabod is absent, God is absent.

REALMS OF GLORY

The earth shall be filled with the knowledge of The glory of the Lord as the waters cover the sea. *(Habakkuk 2:14)* God wants the knowledge of who He is to permeate and cover the entire earth just as the waters cover the sea. He wants His children to manifest His presence, power and glory throughout the entire nations of the earth.

Time must be intentionally dedicated to cultivating the presence of God; seeking His face, learning His scent, knowing His fragrance and aroma. Once you have immersed yourself in Him, you will begin to experience various realms of glory, beyond the imaginable.

20 Now unto him that is able to do exceeding abundantly above all that we ask or think, according to the power that worketh in us, (Ephesians 3:20)

As you yield yourself to trusting Him, He automatically trusts you with more of who He is and what He desires to do. You begin to experience His attributes and learn more about His character.

Water covers over 70% of the earth and, interestingly, our bodies also consist of over 70% of water. God, in His infinite wisdom, uses water as a prophetic symbolism to point us to how the Holy Spirit must be in control of our lives in a greater proportion than anything else.

God took great care in creating man in His own image and likeness. After God formed man from the dust of the earth, He breathed into him and man became a living soul *(Gk–nephesh)*

Man became a living, functioning being; thinking, suggesting, preferring, acting, feeling, desiring and even choosing as he desires. Other created beings do not possess, or enjoy these privileges. For example animals operate or act on instinct while angels only respond to the commands of the written *(logos)* or spoken *(rhema)* Word of God. Rhema can also represent prophetic declarations or divine revelation from God.

God has released to us His Spirit without measure as an eternal covering. There is a limitless, bountiful flow of anointing that He allows to move through every fiber of our being.

As we continue to spend time with Him, the knowledge of who He is overwhelms our minds, wills, intellects and emotions. We become transformed into His image as our minds are adjusted and renewed day by day.

THE PROPHETIC OVERFLOW

As the body of Christ, the process of our global, spiritual expansion moves us from being stagnated puddles to moving streams, to gushing rivers over running our banks, flowing vibrantly to oceans finding the pathway to deep seas.

We enlarge our spiritual territories from domains to communities, to cities, to countries, to nations, to coasts, to regions and, ultimately, to the entire globe. We become carriers of His glory, effecting positive change worldwide.

INDEX

PROPHETESS DR. MATTIE NOTTAGE BA, MA, DD
MINISTRY PROFILE

Widely endorsed as a prophet to the nations, God has used Dr. Mattie Nottage to captivate audiences around the world through her insightful, life-changing messages.

Dr. Nottage is married to Apostle Edison Nottage. She co-pastors, along with her husband, Believers Faith Outreach Ministries, International in Nassau, Bahamas.

Mantled with an uncanny spirit of discernment and an undeniable prophetic anointing, Dr. Nottage is a well-respected international preacher, prolific teacher, motivational speaker, life coach, playwright, author, gospel recording artist and revivalist. She is the President and Founder of *Mattie Nottage Ministries, International, The Global Dominion Network Empowering Group of Companies, The Youth In Action Group and The Faith Village For Girls Transformation Program. She is also The Chancellor of The Mattie Nottage School of Ministry. She is the Founder of the prestigious Mattie Nottage Outstanding Kingdom Woman's Award.*

Dr. Nottage has ministered the gospel, in places such as: Ireland, Brazil, Africa, The Netherlands, throughout the United States of America and The Caribbean. Gifted with an authentic anointing, God uses her to "set the captive free" and to fan the flames of revival throughout the nations. Dr. Mattie Nottage, has an endearing passion to train and equip individuals to advance the Kingdom of God and walk in total victory.

She is the author of her bestselling books, **"Breaking The Chains, From Worship to Warfare", "I Refuse To Die" and "Secrets Every Mother Should Tell Her Daughter About Life" Book & Journal.**

Dr. Nottage is also a regular columnist in The Tribune, the national newspaper of the Bahamas. She has also written numerous publications, stage plays and songs, including the #1 smash hit CD Singles, *"I Refuse To Die In This Place!"*, *"The Verdict Is ...Not Guilty!"* and *"I Still Want You!"*

She has regularly appeared as a guest on various television networks including The Trinity Broadcasting Network (TBN), The Word Network, The Atlanta Live TV and The Babbie Mason Talk Show "Babbie's House" amongst others. Additionally, Dr. Mattie Nottage has been featured in several magazine publications such as the Preaching Woman Magazine and the "Gospel Today" Magazine as one of America's most influential pastors. She, along with her husband, Apostle Edison are the hosts of their very own television show, "Transforming Lives" which airs weekly on The Impact Network.

Dr. Nottage is the former Chairman of the National Youth Advisory Council to the government of the Bahamas and was also recognized and awarded a *"Proclamation of State" by the Mayor and Commissioner of Miami-Dade County, Florida* for her exemplary community initiatives that bring transformation and empowerment to the lives of youth and families globally.

Further, Dr. Nottage has earned her, Bachelor of Arts degree in Christian Counseling, a Masters of Arts degree in Christian Education, and a Doctor of Divinity degree from the renown St. Thomas University, in Jacksonville, Florida and is also a graduate of Kingdom University. Additionally, she has earned her Certified Life Coaching Degree from the F. W. I. Life Coach Training Institute.

Dr. Mattie Nottage is known as a Trailblazer and a *"Doctor of Deliverance"* who is committed and dedicated to *Breaking Chains and Transforming Lives*!

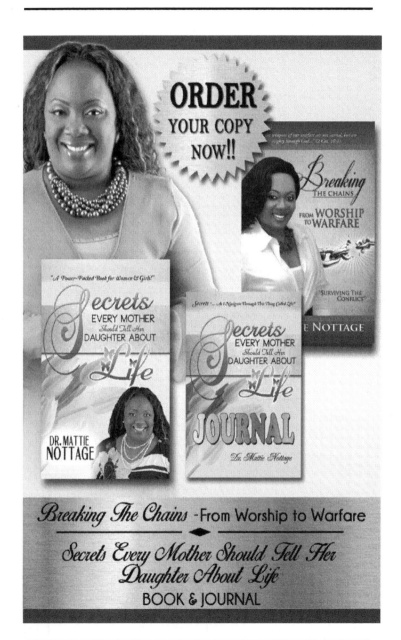

Also Available

Music CD

Music CD Single "I Refuse To Die"
This prophetic song of hope and healing
is an anthem to encourage you to live a life
of victory overcoming every challenge or
adversity of the enemy. Get your copy today
and make a prophetic declaration through song
that you "Refuse To Die!"

Prayer CD

**Prayer of Deliverance
for the
Wounded Soul**

PRAYER OF
DELIVERANCE
for the
WOUNDED
Soul

Dr. Mattie Nottage

PROPHETIC
BREAKTHROUGH PRAYER
BREAKING THE
SPIRIT OF
LIMITATION

DR. MATTIE NOTTAGE

**Breaking the Spirit
of Limitation**

To request Dr. Mattie Nottage for a speaking engagement, upcoming event, life coaching seminar, mentorship session or to place an order for products, please contact:

Mattie Nottage Ministries, International (Bahamas Address)
P.O. Box SB-52524
Nassau, N. P. Bahamas
Tel/Fax: (242) 698-1383 or
(954) 237-8196

OR

Mattie Nottage Ministries, International (U.S. Address)
6511 Nova Dr., Suite #193
Davie, Florida 33317

Tel/Fax: **(888) 825-7568**
UK Tel: 44 (0) 203371 9922

OR

www.mattienottage.org

Follow us on:
Facebook @ DrMattie Nottage
and Twitter **@ DrMattieNottage**

Printed in Great Britain
by Amazon

58212520R00093